Voices from Paradise

The author

Voices from Paradise

How the dead talk to us

Judith Chisholm

JON CARPENTER

Our books may be ordered from bookshops or (post free) from
Jon Carpenter Publishing, Alder House, Market Street, Charlbury,
England OX7 3PH

Please send for our free catalogue

Credit card orders should be phoned or faxed to 01689 870437
or 01608 811969

First published in 2000 by
Jon Carpenter Publishing
Alder House, Market Street, Charlbury, England OX7 3PH
☎ 01608 811969

The photographs on the cover are by Raymond Cass (voice printout) and
Victor Chisholm (Paul)

ISBN 1 897766 59 9

Printed in England by J. W. Arrowsmith Ltd., Bristol

Contents

Foreword

Judith Chisholm's eldest son, Paul, died on 27 August 1992. He died in the night, suddenly and unexpectedly. Paul's funeral took place at Southwark Cathedral but she failed to get the spiritual support and comfort from the Church that she desperately needed. In answer to her question, 'Is there a heaven?', one (unnamed) diocesan bishop replied: 'Oh yes, there must be. Yes, I should think so.' Not much help from that quarter.

However, that painful time was interspersed with unexpected experiences and messages from family and friends. And it was these, among the humdrum events of living, house redecoration, and other day to day events, that told her and her second son, Vic, that Paul was still 'alive' and trying to reassure them of this fact.

They went to mediums, and in the following year came across what is now known as the Electronic Voice Phenomenon, in which voices are imprinted onto tape recordings by methods still not understood forty years after their discovery by Friedrich Jürgenson in Sweden. She experimented and was convinced of their veracity.

This book is therefore a record of Judith's bereavement, anguish and voyage of discovery. It will surely give comfort to many who are travelling or have travelled through 'the valley of the shadow of death' and help them reach the other end, to an understanding that life and human personality continue after death, and there will ultimately be a joyous reunion.

Colin Smythe

The end of the beginning

Something woke me. I looked at the clock. It was 4.45 am. Through the uncurtained bedroom window I could see faint light stealing into a sombre, unsettled sky. A few birds twittered desultorily. It was August 27th 1992. I lay there for a few moments wide awake, alert, wondering why, then got out of bed and for no particular reason decided to go and look at my eldest son Paul who was sleeping downstairs with his girlfriend Tanya.

As I went cautiously down the stairs of the unfamiliar house, every bare wooden step protested loudly. Yesterday, with great effort, I'd ripped off each of the seventeen steps one layer of filthy old yellowish carpet and two layers of pitted brown linoleum, gripped by innumerable 3-inch nails and rusty tacks. Paul had been up the scaffolding at the front, painting the carved wooden spire which crowned the gable of the Victorian house. He painted it green. He decided to start right at the top of the house and work his way down the outside to prevent further decay, before doing anything inside. The North London house was decrepit. We'd recently bought it at auction and were reno-vating it. We were living on a building site but didn't mind; it was exciting.

The door of the room they were sleeping in was partially open. I put my head round it and heard heavy breathing. This was Paul; he often snored, espe-cially if he lay on his back. On camping holidays, when he was younger, I would whistle when the snoring got unbearable and he'd wake up just enough to turn on his side and stop snoring. He was lying on his back. I could just about see in the dim light. He was at one end of the bed and Tanya at the other; both fast asleep. She slept noiselessly. I stood looking at them. A trace of anxiety crept into my mind. His breathing was somehow too heavy, slightly uneven. I hesitated, wondering whether to wake him, but the girl's presence was inhibiting. Surely, sleeping so close, she'd wake up if anything was wrong. He'd told me she slept so lightly she'd often been unnerved to wake up suddenly in the middle of the night to see her sitting there, unable to sleep, looking at him. 'Like a witch!' he'd laughed. Everything was normal. Last night they'd been out for a drink. Tanya was supposed to be cooking dinner, but they were so late, I'd gone out for fish and chips to the end of the road. Paul wasn't hungry. He'd arrived home with gifts. He always brought something. This time it was a huge water melon and a full-length mirror. The mirror was propped in a corner of the room, beginning to reflect the pale grey light of day. I looked at them again, both sleeping then, satisfied, went back to bed.

'Paul won't wake up! Paul won't wake up!' The terrified shriek ripped through my sleep. In an instant I was at the bottom of the stairs. Paul was naked, lying on the floor on his back with his arms straight down at his sides. He looked asleep, his eyes slightly open, turned towards the top of his head. Tanya was crouched over him screaming, 'Wake up Paul! Wake up! He won't wake up. Why won't he wake up?' We looked at each other in blind panic. An ambulance! Quick! Get an ambulance! She threw herself at the phone. I took his shoulders and shook him, begging him to wake up. His flesh felt warm. I was embarrassed by his nakedness. *He must be embarrassed too, but he won't wake up. Wake up – please please wake up!* Parallel images flash through my mind. *My little Paul. The small boy who was so shy of his body he'd never take his clothes off on the beach. Never even roll his sleeves up.* Naked! I'd never seen him naked since he was a little boy. I could not look properly at him. *Why didn't I call an ambulance last night? Why did I come down to look at him? Instinct – mother's instinct, or God? Why did he let me walk away? A mirror! I must get a mirror to check his breathing, someone said that once or I read it. My handbag. Where? Panic. Every moment counts. You must breathe quickly or you're brain damaged. His face is peaceful, lips apart showing his broken front tooth. He isn't cold. Wake up Paul, please please I beg you. God, if you are there, help me.* Tanya's shouting, screaming instructions at me. Breathe into his mouth, pinch his nostrils, press his chest. Count. Release. I am doing it, I did it. I think I did it. Her stark white frantic face. She is gabbling. I don't know what she's saying. Both of us frantic with fear. *Time's running out. He's got green paint on his right thumb.* This is not happening.

The ambulance outside. I fling a coat over my nightdress. Green figures bending over him. A machine thumping his chest. He's still naked on the floor. *My little one. Don't die. Don't leave us.* Humps in the road slow the ambulance down. A red blanket over him. *I had a red blanket over me in the ambulance taking me to the maternity hospital in Hampstead when he was born. The driver told me it was the same blanket which had covered the man shot outside a pub, last Easter by the last woman to be hanged in England, Ruth Ellis – he said it was so as not to show the blood. He thought he was cheering me up. I was sick. Perhaps that is the real reason – not to show the blood. Blood on the carpet.* But there is no blood. Like a lamb, stretched out, neat, still. My Paul, my Paul. All is confusion, distorted, nothing makes sense. Nothing is real. A nurse with red hair comes into the white bare hospital room. She looks solemn. She lays a hand on my arm. I hear a woman screaming 'No, No, No' over and over again. I think the woman is me. Afterwards a blur. I remember vomiting in the hospital grounds.

The three of us sat in the room on the floor huddled round a low table. Victor, my other son, had been phoned at work. I must have phoned him, I couldn't remember. He worked as an electrician in the Signals Department of London Underground. His face was grey. He said he knew something was terribly wrong as soon as the Section Foreman walked along the platform. He thought it was me. 'Do you remember the face I saw in the lino on my kitchen floor?' he asked. I did remember. He had phoned me two days before and told me about the distressed face which had appeared before his eyes in the pattern of the vinyl floor covering. He told me the face wouldn't go, that it was crying and that he himself had begun to cry, hugging the washing machine and saying out loud, 'I love you.' He had related this story feeling rather foolish, wondering what it meant. Then he had suddenly asked for Paul: 'Is Paul there? It doesn't feel as if he's there.' I assured him Paul and Tanya were both sitting opposite me and Vic said again: 'It feels as if he's not there.'

The hours crept by. It grew dark. We didn't move. We were locked together in an intensity of grief which, for the most part, was wordless. It felt to me as though the wheels had stopped turning; a gear had changed in eternity. I was being dragged into a dark empty future by a powerful force, one with whom I'd had no previous dialogue and could not imagine ever coming to terms with. We didn't put the light on. Paul's clothes were still where he had put them when he took them off the night before – on the floor. *The Independent* newspaper of the day before was still on the table. One half page of it was covered in blue biro sketches of ideas for the kitchen layout. He'd sat at the table last night – *last night! What agony! Only last night* – he had pressed hard with the pen sketching frantically. 'Leave me alone,' he'd demanded, 'I haven't got much time.' *'I haven't got much time'. Did he know how much time he had? Nine hours. Can I take cruel time and turn it back? Can this just be a bad dream? Let it be.* Was this why for weeks he'd been saying to me, 'Trust me!' Over and over again. He didn't need to say that. I trusted him completely, except with alcohol. He couldn't handle drink, like his father, my ex-husband, now a no-turning-back alcoholic. Intelligent, charming, quick-witted, creative men who changed in front of your eyes drink by drink into cunning, destructive, frightening men who were pathetically sorry the next day for the damage they'd done. At least Paul was always sorry and I was always happy to forgive him. I loved him.

I was only seventeen when he was born. A big baby, over nine pounds. He ruined my figure. I was skinny and they didn't believe in trying to prevent stretch marks in those days. *Oh, Paul where are you? My best friend, my ally, protector, my brother.* He told everyone I was his sister as I looked so young for so long. I think it was in his psyche from the beginning. I remember one time when he was only about five and someone rang up for me. Paul answered the phone in his squeaky childish voice and the caller asked: 'Are you her sister?' to which he replied 'No, I'm her brother.' *I need you Paul. Everyone needs you. You are the arch keeping the uprights standing. We will fall without you.* What day is it? What time us it? Someone went out to get some food. A bottle of Cognac appeared on the table. We drank it. We didn't get drunk. Tanya sobbed quietly clutching Paul's tee-shirt to her face. I can't remember crying.

Vic picked things up and put them down aimlessly. His beautiful blue eyes were pools of pain. When he was four his teacher said she could drown in his eyes. Joseph Conrad's book *Heart of Darkness* with the corner of page 43 turned down, lay on the floor near the book-case. I remembered this was something Paul was upset about yesterday; he couldn't find his book. Yet here

it was. What a poignant title. We were all staring into the heart of darkness. Vic who was near the book-case knelt down and picked up the book then said in surprise: 'Look at that! Did Paul arrange these books?' 'Yes,' I said and looked where he was pointing. In the midst of dozens of books, most standing upright, three books had been placed one on top of the other. From top to bottom their titles read *Survive, Judith, I've Got your Lucky Number.* How strange! Did it mean when I was going

Judith with Paul, age 6.

to die? Again the question 'Did he know without knowing he knew, what was going to happen?' tugged at my mind.

Some people arrived. I think it must have been the next day though I can't remember going to bed. They looked shocked, offered condolences. Friends of Paul's perched awkwardly in a row on an uncomfortable sofa that needed re-upholstering, their hands clasped stiffly. Words, sentences, intended to comfort. Misery. Gorbie our Siamese cat sat solidly between two of them, staring straight ahead as they were. How did they know what had happened? Someone must have phoned them. I caught Gorbie's blue eye. He knew too. Teas were handed round, half drunk, and left. Cigarettes lit and stubbed out. Yesterday, or whenever it was; the last day of proper life, when I went to get fish and chips for us all, I'd looked up at the high sky piled with ominous clouds and a sentence came sharply into my mind: 'Soon I'll be free of all of this.' It was as though someone had spoken it to me. I thought at that moment I was perhaps going to die, but I didn't mind. I only cared about the shock it would be for my two sons. But it wasn't me. Paul had so often said 'I'll go before you. I couldn't bear if if you died.' Did he know? Last night – or when-ever it was – he'd started to come upstairs but I was getting undressed. He said, 'It doesn't matter.' Was it to say 'Goodbye?' My heart is breaking.

It was a holiday weekend. Late summer holiday in the UK except Scotland: Monday 31st August 1992. My memories of that day and those other dimly lit days are few and fragmented. Perhaps a pain limitation mech-anism of the mind. Paul, my son, lay in the hospital mortuary. We sat around, listlessly, zombified, waiting for the awful joyless holiday weekend to pass. I must have fed the cats, we had three, but I don't remember. I don't remember whether we ate anything or even, whether we went to bed. All I can remember is drinking brandy which didn't do a thing. It didn't blot out inces-sant searching through mental records for answers, for reasons. *I remember your eyes Paul on that last night of life. They were like shattered fragments of blue glass. You said you felt tired. But that was normal; you had been drinking, although you weren't drunk. You looked drawn. But Paul you must understand. It was so diffi-cult to know with you. You hid so much. Did I really know you? Forgive me. Forgive me. I should have done something. You are my son. My eldest son. I love you. I should have called an ambulance. But you would have been so angry if everything had been all right. How could I know?*

Victor and I went to the mortuary to see him for the last time. I didn't want to go but Vic said I would be sorry later if I didn't. I have an impression of clouds racing across a troubled sky but I'm not sure which window I saw them through. We sat side by side, stiff and trance-like staring out of the mortuary's waiting-room window. I vaguely remember some other people leaving the room – a couple; he with his arm round her; she crying into a handkerchief. A solemn-faced man motioned us to enter. A bowl of flowers. Purple cloth covering him, draped over him on a high table. Blotched purple round the top of his head. Vic and I stood side by side, paralysed, unable to say anything, unable to do anything. Mute, motionless. Neither of us kissed him. I don't think either of us touched him. His arms were outside the purple cloth. I saw the green paint was still on his thumb. This body wasn't him. Paul had gone.

When we got back to the house, standing in the shadow of the scaffolding which covered the whole of its front, it seemed unbelievable that a few days before I'd stood in the same spot looking up at Paul balanced precariously on a loose plank. If the plank had been secure he would have been balancing on one that wasn't – he was like that. I visualised him again, paint brush in hand, at a height which would have given me vertigo, shouting instructions to Tanya and me co-opted as extra painters for the fiddly lower bits. I looked at the carved wooden spire on the gable. The last thing he'd painted. It reached towards heaven. We walked miserably through to the back of the house where the kitchen would be; the bathroom, the little study. All was bare, rough old brick, tarpaulin, bags of cement, dust. A sudden wind tugged furiously at the tarpaulin covering a garden door opening. It heaved heavily up and down several times. We looked quickly at the nearby trees to see if a gale was blowing up. They were perfectly still.

The next day, Vic went home briefly. He shared a flat with his fiancée in south-east London. When he returned in the evening, he walked in without a word, sat down and put his head in his hands. I asked him what was wrong. He shook his head in disbelief. Finally he told me the flat had been empty when he arrived. He found a note by the bed from her. She wrote that she had left him. She had got another boyfriend with whom she was staying and would he make arrangements to pay his share of the mortgage on the flat and the telephone bill. All her clothes had gone as well as large pieces of furniture. The jewellery he had given her including her engagement ring was left in a tangle on the bedside table with the note. He really loved that girl and I felt enormous pity for him – and rage. How could she be so crass as to kick him when he was so far down? Surely he didn't deserve it. And if he did – who was I to know the secrets of their relationship? – couldn't a better time have been chosen to deliver such a body blow? Together Vic and I sank to an all-time low.

The funeral was on September 4th: the service at Southwark Cathedral, burial at Highgate Cemetery. Arranging it all was unreal. I could not reconcile hearing myself on the phone speaking in a business-like way about what needed to be done to deal with the remains of my own child. I could hear myself saying: 'Oh, yes, thank you. What time will that be? Shall I send a cheque or pay by credit card?' but I was screaming *'Why? Why him? Don't leave us. Please come back!'* yet no-one heard or replied. Victor had nothing suitable to wear. He rushed out to buy a dark suit and black tie in a local store. I found some black clothes in my wardrobe. I had lost so much weight, the skirt swivelled round my waist and had to be kept in place with a safety pin. Flowers

Vic in the garden of our house, September 1997.

bobbed up and down on the coffin as we followed the hearse in stately procession. I felt numb. Shining chrome ahead. Stiff backs. A beautiful day, sunny with a playful wind that twirled golden autumn leaves in the gutter, some people crossing themselves as we passed. There were four of us in the car. Victor of course and Tanya. *After the funeral, she will have to leave.* I blamed her rightly or wrongly for Paul's death. I couldn't even bear to look at her.

The cathedral was full of dark clad people, most of whom I didn't know. Paul's friends. He loved people. Once friends, they were for life. Andrea, an ex-girlfriend, was there with her mother and brother. A jolly postcard had arrived from her whilst on holiday, when Paul was in the mortuary. She was distraught; blaming herself for having been away when it happened. We were handed the Order of Service. The coffin was borne in to the Hallelujah Chorus. Fred, the chief pall-bearer, one of Paul's school-friends, white with misery. Later all he said to me was: 'I was going to a football match with him later this week.' Close family was led to the front pew: turning, I saw my brother Gerald and sister Dora behind. I was very glad they'd come.

Paul was the pariah of the family. A non-conformist who offended their innate conservatism. He drank – more than one glass of sherry. He fought, both physically and for his principles. He worked when necessary, usually on a building site: hard physical work, then he'd spend what he earned on presents for people and rounds of drinks. He was streetwise and highly intelligent – an intellectual rough diamond. Once at the age of eighteen, on a round Europe train trip, he came home from Paris just for a bath and left again for Paris immediately after it. Another day he arrived home with a huge bronze head which had been placed on a plinth in a small London square ready to be cemented in place after a short official ceremony. I can't remember in whose image the head was. A number of people were standing around waiting for the ceremony to begin when Paul walked by in workmen's clothes, picked the head up on the spur of the moment and marched off. No-one said a word. Presumably they thought he'd gone for the cement. I was horrified when he presented me with it. He said he'd done it as a test of people's psychological reactions, but there weren't any. We didn't know what to do with the thing and finally decided to take it back to the square it was intended for which we did by car, in the dead of night. Strangely enough it was never assembled. The whole thing, plinth, head and all simply disappeared. And this was the same boy who'd jumped off a bus when he saw a woman being mugged in the street by four men, chased them, and retrieved her handbag, getting a broken jaw for his trouble. It was wired up for weeks and he could only take liquid food through a straw in the side of his mouth. In fact nearly every bone in his body was broken at some stage in his life through doing bad or doing good.

The canon is saying something. My eyes stray to the coffin covered with a cloth. *No, he's not there. Look at something else.* I fix my eyes on pennants with crosses hanging from the vaulted ceiling. *My family never understood him. It got to the point where they talked about their children who were lawyers and other clever things but I never talked about Paul who was so much more than clever for fear of the look of quizzical disapproval and pity for me which would pass over their faces.* We are motioned to stand up. Opening chords are played. We sing *All Things Bright and Beautiful. I am back in infant school; four years old: our teacher at the piano, hands high over the keys, body swivelled to face us, singing with us encouragingly without looking at her hands* All creatures great and small, *me with an eye on the small bottles of milk in a crate in the corner of the classroom. After the hymn we'd all have to drink one. I hate that milk. It's always warm and sickly.* The singing has ended. My heart leaps into my throat and thuds back into my chest. I hear it like the huge, muffled beat of a drum. I am acutely aware of Victor's suffering. We exchange a glance. He's being motioned to take his place at the lectern. We are each reading a poem. His is *Conclusion* by Sir Walter Raleigh:

> Even such is time that takes in trust
> Our youth, our joys, and all we have
> And pays us but with age and dust.
> Who in the dark and silent grave
> When we have wandered all our ways
> Shuts up the story of our days
> And from which earth and grave and dust
> The Lord shall raise him up I trust.

He reads it perfectly, even raising his eyes to look at the congregation before delivering the last line. I applaud him silently. As he steps down, music begins. It's *Mr. Know it All* by Stevie Wonder. Paul loved Stevie Wonder. It's strange to see it written in the Order of Service – 'Tape Song – *Mr. Know it All.*' Tanya chose it. She said it summed Paul up. It did somehow. He did know it all. He knew it all from the age of nought, *but he didn't know how to stay alive, did he? He lived in the fast lane and crashed. But perhaps he didn't want to live, to be old. Shall I ever know?* We listen to the sweet melody. It's painful to focus on the words, they are too poignant. People stand silently and sadly. I catch sight of my former husband, Paul's father. He looks stricken and very old. I see he has his second ex-wife with him. It's a long time since I saw her and I notice her hair has gone completely grey. She is wearing a loud check jacket. Now it's my turn to read. My heart misses a beat. My poem is W. B. Yeats' *He Wishes for the Cloths of Heaven.* I avert my eyes from the coffin. It's unbelievable to think that Paul, my full-of-life Paul, so wise, so intelligent, my son – is in that. As I step up to the lectern, I see the canon standing in the shadows to my left. I wonder if he has had such a service in the cathedral before – poems and pop songs. I put on my glasses. They tip sideways on my face – one of the little screws fell out of the left arm some time in my former life. So I have to read with one hand holding them on:

> Had I the Heavens' embroidered cloths
> Enwrought with golden and silver light,
> The blue and the dim and the dark cloth,
> Of Night and Light and the Half Light
> I would spread the cloths under your feet
> But I being poor have only my dreams.
> I have spread my dreams under your feet.
> Tread softly because you tread on my dreams.

As I read I can vaguely see people's upturned faces. The beautiful words reach into the cathedral, but my voice sounds thin and childish.

Trust me

'She's a junkie, didn't you know?' I looked at Richard, one of Paul's crowd, blankly. *Tanya a junkie!* 'Do you mean she's taking drugs?' He returned my gaze incredulously. 'Where've you been for the last twenty years? Her husband got her hooked. Look at her, she's so shot up she's got nowhere else left to put it. Paul felt sorry for her, he wanted to get her off it but he tried it too – heroin.' *Heroin! Paul would have done that, of course, he tried everything. Was that the explanation for some spoons I'd discovered hidden behind a sofa? They looked as though they'd had syrup or toffee in them which had been burned and blackened.* How could I be so stupid? I just had no interest in or knowledge of drugs and the drug culture. And I didn't even know Tanya had been – or was still – married.

She was someone Paul had met thirteen years earlier in Nottingham and had re-encountered by one of those quirks of fate when they both took shelter from the rain in the same North London pub earlier in the year. I gazed round the crowded pub in Highgate where most of us had gathered after the interment at Highgate Cemetery, catching sight of her with a group of other people; blonde hair falling in wisps from her pony tail round a chalk white face above a stick-like body. She was attractive, but very very thin. How come I hadn't noticed that before? Perhaps she'd lost some weight over these last few dreadful days.

Richard followed my gaze. His voice cut in again: 'She put something in his drink that night. Didn't want him to leave her. She's jealous of every other woman, even you.' I suddenly felt faint. 'How do you know?' Did you see her do it? What was it?' I demanded. A vision of going to the police and accusing her of murder flashed through my mind. How could it be proved? Was what Richard had said even true? A group of people eddied towards us. I didn't know them, but they obviously knew Richard and he, by accident or design, was swept into their wake. In any case, I don't think he intended to answer my questions. I pushed my way through the crowd towards the ladies room to be alone for a few minutes, Pubs were not my scene at the best of times, and this was not the best of times. I felt like lying down and dying. 'Oh, Judy, Judy!'

Tanya was in there. She held out her arms and clasped me in them. I felt her bony thigh against me. She was cold and clammy. I pulled away. 'Look Tanya,' I burst out 'You'll have to leave the house. Vic and I want to be alone.' It was probably not the time nor the place to deliver this line. But I'd never rehearsed this part before. 'Oh, no, no. Don't get rid of me.' She leaned on the wall and slowly, dramatically, slid down it clasping her head in her hands. My son was dead. I looked at her without even seeing her, and walked out.

We were finally alone, with our thoughts. It was 2 am on September 5th – the morning after the funeral. Vic and I sat on the sofa, the one that needed re-upholstering. Everything felt so strange, so empty. Paul's clothes were still on the floor where he had tossed them. Nothing had been touched. Several empty brandy bottles were stacked in the hearth. Vic picked one up and tilted it hopefully. No luck! Neither of us had drunk alcohol in the pub. It would have been good to have a drink now. The moon was shining through the uncurtained windows. We didn't switch on the light. We didn't speak. Both of us were facing a new future – Vic without his brother and his fiancée, me without my eldest son. Death could snatch away, at an instant, all that was familiar, safe and reassuring.

I sneaked a sidelong look at Vic. What if something happened to him? That would be the end for me too. I had a macabre image of strangling the three cats first (who'd look after them?) and laying their bodies out side by side next to mine as I slipped into unconsciousness.

Suddenly, to our horror, we saw a figure silhouetted on the scaffolding outside. It looked like a witch with long streaming hair and thin outstretched arms; claw-like hands clasping the poles.

'My God, it's Tanya,' Vic breathed.

'Don't let her in!' I gasped. 'I can't bear her near me.'

'We can't shut her out' Vic said tensely.

'Yes, we can!' I sprang to pull the curtains, but it was too late. She'd reached the first floor window. It was broken, and she was in. We heard her coming down the bare stairs. 'You must get rid of her.' I clutched Vic's arm. She must leave immediately; it was the most important thing in the world to me at that moment. 'She's got a husband. She must go to him – tonight!'

The door was pushed open. Tanya came in and stood in front of us. She looked awful. Her face was almost green, her hair wild. I later learned she'd collapsed in the pub after we'd left, suffering from withdrawal symptoms. Andrea, Paul's ex-girl friend, had driven her to hospital from where she'd discharged herself, returned to the pub and 'borrowed' £50 from someone for a fix.

'Are you blaming me?' she quavered.

'Well, you didn't help,' I replied.

'It wasn't me,' she wailed 'I didn't do anything. I didn't kill him.'

You didn't wake up when he was dying, you were too drugged and probably had put something in his drink. But now, nothing mattered to me except that she leave us alone. I battened down any emotion that threatened to surface, for or against. It wasn't vindictiveness or revenge. It was a purge. I knew if it didn't happen that night it might not happen at all.

'You've got to go now,' I said.

She rushed over to Paul's clothes and began to scrabble through them, wrenching the belt from his jeans, tossing things around like at a jumble sale. We watched dispassionately. She began to throw clothes in a huge bag she hauled out from under the bed, then suddenly abandoned the task and flopped into a chair.

'Where's his diary?' she demanded.

'I've got it,' I said.

'I want it.'

'No – just phone for a taxi.'

Vic got up. 'Look Tanya,' he said gently. 'You've got to go now. You can't stay here. Paul's gone now.'

She began to weep. 'I'm pregnant,' she said. 'And you're never going to see his baby.' She fixed me with a baleful glare. I didn't believe she was telling the truth and didn't, at that moment, even care.

Vic gave me an agonised look. I felt like a stone. 'Have you got a number for a taxi?' he asked. She fumbled in her bag and drew out a card. He phoned. It took ten minutes for the taxi to arrive. We sat in painful silence. There was nothing more to say. When the taxi driver rang the bell she looked wildly round the room: 'I want that!' She pointed to a pink chaise longue she and Paul had brought back one day. Neither of us reacted. She hesitated, then left, slamming the front door. We didn't turn to look at her departure out of the window but continued to sit, like zombies, on the uncomfortable sofa for most of the rest of the night.

The next day and the days that followed crept up remorselessly behind us, forcing us along, like a malevolent beast watching, waiting to devour us if we weakened. We had to grapple with him daily in order to survive. It would have been so much easier to sink into despondency; to do nothing, to dwell, to grieve, to wonder why us? But it was not possible. Yes, we grieved. Tears came to me at last. They flowed like an open tap – into my tea, onto books, soaking the cats whom I hugged to my chest for comfort. They didn't like their fur being wet, nor the salty taste and hastily licked themselves into shape as soon as I released them. I think the tears even made my typewriter rusty or disabled it in some way, as it behaved in a very peculiar manner during those days: whizzing from side to side like a trapped bird in a cage, with its electronic heart whirring weakly, refusing to obey any commands. It was necessary to try and close the door of the mind that allowed a flow, a torrent of memories to flood through.

Trudging to the Maternity Home up Hampstead High Street, wearing flat, red shoes with square toes that I love, bought from Gamba in Soho, a glamorous specialist shop famous for its ballet shoes. I can't even see my feet when I look down, I'm huge. A petite girl, seventeen years old, with an enormous belly. I know it's a boy. I'm all out in front, that's the sign. John introduces me, in the last stages of pregnancy, to his friend the comedian Spike Milligan from the Goon Show on radio. He's an avid supporter of some football club or the other. He drops his eyes to my middle and says to my husband, 'Aha, this is your centre forward, is it?' It doesn't seem very funny now. It's strange how these insignificant remarks stick in the mind. Deciding what to call my very large nine pound baby: Maurice, after my father? No, doesn't sound right for a baby. Maxwell? I can't imagine how we – or rather I – thought that one up. In the end we fix on Paul. The name means 'Little One'. He never forgave us for not giving him a middle name, but in any case he was usually called by his nickname 'Widge'. John attached that to him. I don't know why, or what it means and I'm not sure John knows either. It stuck anyway. His eyes are so blue, sloping slightly. He looks like the actor Paul Newman when young. Girls fight over him, yet he's somehow pure, almost shy and at the same time tough and streetwise.

Forget it! Forget it! Stop thinking!

An image of a boat, blue sky, white buildings. Menorca! He is sixteen, Vic eleven. I young, divorced, good-looking, carefree, happy. We are all so happy. Like three young friends. Paul is the leader, the instigator, the dare-devil. Vic always apprehensive, half enjoying the escapades, half fearing the outcome. I have supreme confidence in Paul. We hire a rubber dinghy with a motor. He takes the helm. We lie back, soaking up the sun, gazing at the blue sky, loving it. It clouds over. Suddenly we're in huge seas; waves lapping into the boat. We see the landing stage of the old rose-coloured penal colony where prisoners were kept who had yellow fever, but we can't get near it. The sea takes us further and further out. Vic and I both quietly panic but he is confident, sitting on the very edge of the dinghy, smiling, reassuring us. We'll be OK. He's in charge. It takes a long time, and hectic baling, to get back to shore, but we make it. Another adventure. Life with Paul is – was – an adventure.

Stop thinking. Stop! The problem was that in public almost anything could turn my tears on, hard as I tried to stop them flowing. In fact, the more I tried, the more I wept. This ordeal began on the first day I forced myself out of the house when I took all the things Paul had used on those last days to the charity shop. The sight of his bedclothes, the duvet, the pillow, even the casserole dish the last meal had been cooked in, was too much to bear. I made several trips to the Christian Aid shop at the top of the road. I don't know what they thought as I stood at the counter with my arms full of bedding and tears welling up in my eyes. They didn't say anything, though some weeks later, when I'd blurted out what had happened, I received a very kind and well-meaning letter from the manager of the shop. They sold all the things anyway, because each trip I made, the things I'd taken in before had all gone. It's just as well, or the sight of them would have set me off again.

Back home, I gathered his personal things together: a little bundle – he didn't like possessions, he usually gave nearly everything he had away, even clothes. Some cigarette papers, letters, photographs, his diary; how heart-wrenching to see appointments marked in for the days after he'd died. Was there any indication he was ill enough to die? I searched the diary minutely for any clue, feeling guilty. We respected each other's diaries. Tears again. They oozed down the side of my face, painful and itchy in their saltiness and plopped onto the diary's black back.

Vic went back to work on London Underground after a week's compassionate leave. I began work on the house. It was September 8. Sunny, but without warmth. A kind of harsh, white, uncaring light full of the sounds of other people's lives passing me by. Some workmen had been helping Paul with the house – acquaintances of his rather than friends. I decided to call them back to carry on with the heavy work, rather than find an impersonal building contractor. At least they knew him; there was a connection. I needed connections desperately, for comfort. As I was making a plan of action, a plasterer arrived at the door. He had his trade card in his hand. 'Paul asked me to turn up today,' he said.

'Paul's dead,' I said, lips quivering.

The man blanched, and drew back, shocked. 'Oh, no,' he said. 'He can't be. He was all right the last time I saw him – only two weeks ago. I'm very, very sorry. He was a nice man. A good guy.' He left, shaking his head in bewilderment.

I watched him go down the street. *Oh God. Let me undo everything. Let this be a dream. Let me wake up!* An unspoken cry of anguish to a God who'd let this happen and who I wasn't sure I believed in. The plasterer disappeared from view. Too late, I realised I hadn't taken his card.

On the 12th of September, the day before Paul's birthday, Vic and I decided to get out of the house. Work wasn't going well at London Underground for Vic. He couldn't concentrate on the fiddly, intricate mass of components and cables which makes up an electrical signals circuit. He was also doing things round the house after work to help try and get it into a more liveable-in condition. As it was, we were cooking on a stove which stood in the middle of a bare room stripped of its plaster, in the back extension, which was shrouded with plastic as parts of most of the outer walls were being rebuilt. The plastic flapped in the wind, allowing gusts of cold air to eddy round the area. The euphemistically called 'shower room' – a wooden builder's pallet under a sprinkler – was in a corner of the same room, later to be partitioned off. The evening of the day before he died Paul had brought a lamp into this room and with Vic's help put a lintel over a large hole in the wall where french doors would eventually be. Later still that evening, about 11.30, he'd frantically built three-quarters of a brick wall in the extension. It was as though he knew time was running out yet there was so much to do. Significantly, with hindsight, he'd said: 'Vic should come and live here and do what I do.' The twenty-sixth of August – only seventeen days ago. The world was now a different place. That he, Paul, as tough and durable as the heavy lintel he and Vic had hoisted up, had gone, was no more! It was inconceivable.

So, on this evening of the 12th September, we both went out. I to Vic's flat in South East London, to clean and tidy it ready for letting. He felt this was the best way to deal with it as he had decided to live with me for the time being in Islington, yet he still had a mortgage to pay. Vic went to a party in North London. Neither of us had very much enthusiasm for the evening ahead, but we both felt we should get out of the house.

On arrival at his flat, I set about cleaning and arranging it. Hard work, but at least it was a change of scenery. Eventually, tired out, I lay down on a sofa and switched on the television. It was the last night of the Proms at the Albert Hall. I felt utterly depressed. The malevolent beast had me in its grip and I was just about ready to surrender. I was only half watching when suddenly my attention was drawn to what the presenter was saying: 'And now the Scots Piper plays. He is wearing Chisholm of Strathglass tartan.' Our tartan! I have never seen it worn by a piper at the Proms before. I felt he was wearing it especially for Paul. Tired though I was, it was impossible to sleep. At about 5.30 am the phone rang. I leapt out of bed, heart thumping. It was Vic.

'I'm coming over there,' he said. 'I can't stay in the house; I've had too much of a shock.' When he arrived, this is what he told me:

'I decided to go back to the Islington house as the party was closer to it than my flat. I got to the house at about 2 am, got into bed, and immediately fell fast asleep. I was awakened by a ringing sound in my ears which I thought would never stop, and by the sound of the toilet flushing. It was still dark outside. I looked at my watch – a quarter to five in the morning. I shot up in bed, thinking you were back, then realised I was alone in the house. I was panic stricken. I thought someone had broken in. As I listened, I heard the toilet finish flushing, then I heard the sitting room door open and close gently with that little thump it made because of the old layers of draught excluder round it. Then – I heard Paul cough. I know his cough, and I *knew* he was in the sitting room. Then, I heard him cough again – you know the way he does, those little coughs, but quite contented, when he's interested in something. I was absolutely petrified. I couldn't move for ages, then when I finally did get up, I crept downstairs and as I passed the sitting room door I hesitated for a moment thinking, 'Shall I go in?' But I knew he was in there, and that he was leaning with one elbow on the mantlepiece just as he did. And, I just couldn't do it. I couldn't face seeing him in there, so I ran out of the house and all the way down that long street past the builders' yard. There was no-one around, yet I felt sure he was there, running with me, behind me, on the wall, ready to jump down. I've never felt so scared in my life. I know I shouldn't have been because he's my brother, but I just couldn't face it.'

This spirit visit by Paul, on his birthday, to his brother – because that's what we believe it was – proved to be the beginning of a long road of psychic unfolding which Vic and I are both still on. At the time, knowing nothing about such things and being sceptics, we searched for a more prosaic answer to the night's events. But there was none. Vic knew what he heard, and heard what he knew – and that was that. I believed his story: I had no reason not to. And on hearing it, a tiny spark of hope ignited in my breast. Was there something else? Dare I think so? For the second night in less than three weeks, we sat side by side on the sofa till well past daybreak, but this time we had something to talk about.

October 2. The men came – four of them. Building work began again. The house filled up with more bags of cement, sheets of plasterboard, cartons of nails, ladders, scaffolding, picks, shovels – and dust, which floated in the air in a continuously descending pall of grimy whiteness. I was now the reluctant and inexperienced foreman, phoning for supplies: Carlite Bonding; bag after bag of the dreadful pink stuff seemed to be consumed, and most of it, though intended for the walls, finished up on the floor – every floor – tramped round by heavy boots, and cats' paws. It was delivered by a very grumpy driver who could never find a space in the heavily parked street to stop his van which made him even more angry. I was sent out to buy unfamiliar things like a Stillson's pipe grip, brass olives, long nosed pliers' and a diamond scraper. This last item I was to become very familiar with, using it day after day, week after weary

The house in Islington.

week to scour and winkle out countless layers of yellow, grey, cream, green, red paint and sticky brown varnish from beautiful Victorian Rose pitch pine doors and panelling and the intricate mouldings of mahogany bannisters and stair-rods.

Each evening I paid the men their day's wages. I eventually realised this 'daily rate' business, suggested by them, was not a good arrangement when I overheard Watery-eyed John (a very apt name given one of them by Paul) say to Young Ted:

'I'm running out of work,' and the reply: 'String it out mate, make it last.' I'd been naive enough to believe they had more respect for Paul's memory than that!

One evening soon after work on the house had started again, a curious incident occurred. Vic and I were both out. When we returned, late, I listened for messages on the telephone answering machine. There was only one. It occupied the whole of the tape. It was a very unpleasant call from my ex-husband John who was drunk and as a result, abusive. The parts of the tape where he hadn't been speaking he'd filled with what sounded like foreign language radio broadcasts and other meaningless stuff. At the end, after he'd rung off (I could hear his phone being put down), the answering machine carried on recording, turning itself on and off, on and off several times. Then there was the sound of a phone ringing. It was picked up and John's voice said 'Yes' aggressively. There was silence. He said 'Yes' a second time, a little less aggressively, and then 'Who's there?' in a very worried tone. After a few seconds I heard the sound of his receiver being replaced and the tape on our answering machine cut off. So, the telephone had somehow phoned John back after his call, by itself, and recorded itself doing it. I was very surprised as I'd never heard of a phone making a call on its own initiative. It was very tempting to think that perhaps Paul in spirit had been witness to this nasty call from his father and, not liking what he heard, phoned him back. But not wishing to read something paranormal into every out-of-the-ordinary experience, I simply stored this one away in my memory bank. Later I was able to put this strange return phone call into context.

Half way through October, for no reason other than that grieving seems to progress in this way, roller-coasting from a high of near normality to a new low, I became very depressed indeed; full of regrets, remorse, blaming myself, crying almost continually, so much so that I made Vic very depressed too. He was feeling pretty bad on his own account, which made me feel even worse.

We agreed we should find a local church which would perhaps ease the pain and give us some comfort and maybe hope. Not being regular church-goers we felt a little guilty about this; calling on God when you're in trouble and forgetting Him when you're not. Vic was more religious than I. He at least had been a member of the Methodist Church but had left when they informed him it was sinful to live with a woman before marriage. He said he thought there were more important issues for the Church to address than his domestic arrangements. Anyway, we were in the middle of discussing

Church, when lo and behold, a leaflet dropped through the letterbox from St. Thomas' Church, Finsbury Park – just around the corner. Printed on the back of the leaflet were the words: '2nd November: A Service for the Dead'. We decided to go to it.

St. Thomas' is Anglican high church, built of red brick and cosy. As we walked in, I felt tears welling up again. I knew if anyone was pleasant to me I'd break down. A sidesman who watched us come in was very welcoming. He had a lovely friendly face. He greeted us and showed us where to sit. It was very difficult to stop my lips from quivering. In fact, having sat down one row from the front, I could see the vicar only through a blur of unshed tears. I just about discerned that he had a boyish face and grey hair. I could feel him looking at me quizzically. I must have looked grotesque with a screwed-up face and puffy eyes. But I expect he'd seen it all before. My nose needed blowing badly, but I could only blow it when the responses got loud. Neither Vic nor I knew the responses and we both felt quite foolish standing there dumbly with incense wafting round. The incense was so overpowering and I wondered how the vicar and the choristers managed to inhale it every day and still stay on their feet.

The diocesan bishop was taking part of the service that evening. He was a tall man, red-faced and wearing a purple sash round his waist. He looked very imposing. After the service we all went into the vestry for tea and, feeling desperate, I edged up to him, tea cup in hand. 'Is there really a Heaven?' I asked. He looked down at me in mild irritation: 'Oh, yes – there must be. Yes, I should think so,' was his reply. Then he moved away to talk to someone else. Somehow or other that seemed to be a very unsatisfactory answer – from a bishop.

We went to church a few more times after this. It was difficult to ignore the bell on Wednesdays for evening service as we were close and it was loud. We felt we were being summoned personally, and having started to go we ought to continue. Besides, Stephen, the vicar, was very pleasant. He lived a couple of streets away and one afternoon I went to his house, by arrangement, to talk about my bereavement. It's strange, but all I can remember from that afternoon are the green walls and ceiling of his sitting room. They were a vibrant organic deep blue-green like a swamp in shadow made by bright sunlight. I'd never seen such an invasive colour on the walls of a house before and it penetrated my consciousness to the point where I couldn't concentrate properly on anything else. But I was grateful at least to have been able to talk to him. After a while, Church palled on us and we went less and less until we stopped completely – going only at Christmas. If I happened to meet Stephen on the street or in the local newsagents, I felt very bad about this, like a deserter from the army deserving to be shot, especially as he invariably smiled sweetly and addressed me by my Christian name.

One day Frank, a friend of Paul's, phoned. He told me Paul had visited him two nights ago in spirit. I was stunned by this statement. Frank is a non-believer of the firmest kind. A total cynic, someone whom everyone referred to as a 'hard man'. Definitely not the kind to believe in ghosts. He said he had been asleep in bed. He woke up suddenly and saw Paul dressed in jeans and jumper standing at the foot of his bed, smiling – the crooked smile Paul had. Frank said he looked straight at him for a few moments, not shocked as he thought he was dreaming. He closed his eyes, opened them again and Paul was still there. He remained there for several seconds – or minutes (Frank said it was hard to judge how much time had passed) – and then slowly faded. This was an impressive confession from someone like Frank, and completely unexpected. It gave us much food for thought and made me envious. I wished Paul would visit me.

Neither Vic nor I had ever been to a medium, but after Frank's experience we decided to try and find one. I asked a friend from Sri Lanka if he knew someone (this particular friend knew everything) and he recommended a Mr. Lister from Walthamstow, not too far from where we lived. I made an appointment with this man. It was around the end of November 1992.

The bus seemed to take for ever. Walthamstow is in the unexplored hinterland of Greater London. We wondered if our stop would ever come. At last it did and we eventually found ourselves in a long street of terraced houses. Mr. Lister's house was almost at the end. A woman with unnaturally black hair opened the door and ushered us in a kindly way into the sitting room. The room was sweltering and the over-riding impression was brown and tan; curtains, carpet and squashy imitation leather chairs. A woman was sitting in one of them and the black-haired woman, whom we later learnt was Mrs. Lister, sat down next to her and immediately resumed the conversation she'd obviously interrupted to open the door. Her talking was a kind of verbal haemorrhaging accompanied by much arm waving and queries of 'Do you know what I mean dear?' We were motioned to sit down by one of the sweeps of her arm, which we did, sinking into the depths of plastic jelly-like chairs which gripped our bodies in a sticky embrace. After sweating for about twenty minutes, Vic asked where Mr. Lister might be. Mrs. Lister indicated a lean-to at the rear of the room and carried on talking. We wondered what on earth he was doing in a lean-to at that time of night, but had no choice but to sit uncomfortably and wait.

Eventually the lean-to door squeaked open and two women and a man emerged. One woman was upset and had her face half-buried in a handkerchief. Mrs. Lister sprang to her feet and ushered the two women into the hall. Mr. Lister (for it was he) indicated we should go into the lean-to. He held open the door. There was not much room and he was a burly man. We all squeezed in and Vic and I sat down on chairs surrounded by gardening implements, and all sorts of other paraphernalia. Mr. Lister leaned against a small table facing us. He only had one arm. The left one was a stump. Obviously conscious of it he explained he'd lost half his arm in an accident with some machinery when he was an engineer, or some such thing. I couldn't help wondering why, if he was so conscious of it, he wore short sleeves. Vic took out a small round box he had brought which contained Paul's tooth – a false one which had fallen out, and which he was intending to get cemented back in, but never did. I felt very emotional and already very let down. The surroundings and the medium were not what I was expecting. Mr. Lister held the tooth for a moment, eyes closed and then said suddenly:

'It's a man. I see you now. There's people with him. He's behind you' – indicating Vic – 'his grandmother and grandfather are with him. He's wearing a hat.'

At this point I burst into tears. Paul often wore hats. They were a trademark of his. The latest he'd been wearing before his death, and one which had actually disappeared off the hallstand – we couldn't find it anywhere – was a black leather pillbox type, the kind that Africans often wear.

Mr. Lister ignored my tears and continued, addressing Vic: 'It's your brother. You've got to carry on. Keep doing the things you're doing. He says he's thirty-four; he's recuperating.' Paul was actually thirty-six but never bothered to remember exactly how old he was and tended, Peter Pan-like, to err on the minus side. Recuperating? That didn't mean anything at the time.

Mr. Lister spoke very rapidly, almost as fast as his wife, and each time he made a statement he flung his stump out to the right and rattled off, 'Can you take that with you dear?' But what he had said was uncannily accurate and I heard myself murmuring, in a choked voice 'He's here.' I even turned to look behind Vic to see if Paul was visible.

Mr. Lister continued talking: 'He's only young. Been dead a short while, two months. He wasn't quite right in the head when he died; the pain was in his chest and stomach.' This was correct. He had died just over two months before. The cause of death was bronchial asthma and an inability to wake up because of having taken drink or drugs (or both) on that last evening. Hence – pain in his chest and stomach, and drugs or drink, make one 'not quite right in the head.'

'His father was very bitter,' Mr. Lister said. 'Even more after he died. You should get his papers back from his father, but you should do it' (indicating Vic), 'not your mother. There's too much bitterness between him and her.'

It was true, we had given some papers to John relating to Paul and some notes he'd made, and wanted them back. And there was a great deal of bitterness between John and me, at least from him to me. I had stopped feeling anything except pity for him a long time before. And how did Mr. Lister know I was Vic's mother? We never said, and Vic and I don't look alike. How did he know all this? I had taken off my wedding ring in order not to give any clues. Other than the tooth, we had given him nothing and told him nothing. Could all this pin-point accuracy be guesswork?

He rattled off more information. It was so fast it was hard to keep track of. He mentioned Paul's flat (he did have a flat of his own) and a house 'being upside down' (obviously ours). Suddenly, it was all over. With the words 'He's fading. Take that away with you dear,' we were ushered into the sitting room again. 'It's £10 please, dear,' he said, holding out his hand. We were so flustered, Vic gave him twenty. But we reckoned it was worth it.

Within seconds we were out on the grey pavement heading for home – elated. On the bus I made notes of all Mr. Lister had said. We agreed the information he had given was remarkable. He'd never seen either of us in his life. The only thing he could have been sure about from my behaviour was that we had lost a close relative, or friend. But that's all. By the time we got home we were a little less elated, and by next morning doubts crept in. Had we given something away? Maybe he could read minds. Was it really all that accurate. Perhaps a little generalised? I referred to my notes. Yes, it was accurate, no we hadn't given anything away. And yet – could a tooth tell him all that?

It was soon the beginning of December. Christmas was looming. Last Christmas had been the best ever. Paul, Vic, Andrea, her mother and I had gone to Crowsley Manor in Hampshire, a brooding majestic pile of a building rented on a long lease for a pittance by some friends of Paul's. Their period of grace was ending soon and this was to be the final Christmas at the Manor, though they themselves were abroad. I had never been to the rambling mansion before and was entranced by the gloom, the huge black and white tiled entrance hall and towering Christmas tree lit by sparkling tiny white lights which they'd arranged before they left. The Manor was straight out of Daphne du Maurier's *Rebecca*. 'Last night I went to Mandalay again...' We all enjoyed the few days there so much. It made a deep impression. It was magical.

Now the seasons had turned again. The magic was gone for good. This Christmas would be very different. Two friends of ours, who had been shocked to hear about Paul, came over from Ireland. Heidi and Helmut, a German couple whom we'd met ten years earlier when, in one of my mad moments, after seeing the film *Ryan's Daughter* shot on the Dingle Peninsula, I'd decided to move to the west of Ireland and found a cottage half way up a mountain two peninsulas down from the Dingle. Heidi and Helmut were neighbours and we became great friends. The scenery in the film looked spectacular and is even better in real life, but the social isolation proved too great and in the end I sold the cottage, but kept half the land. They wanted to visit Highgate Cemetery and see Paul's grave. I hadn't been near the place since the funeral. My pain was too near the surface. But they were keen to go so we went.

As we passed through the huge black iron gates I thought of how much Paul had liked the crumbling Victorian splendour of this place. Proud, grey catacombs now broken and overgrown. Damp, tangled vegetation; overblown headstones bearing fat, wistful cherubs and unctuous angels. Karl Marx is buried in the section of cemetery on the other side of the road. As a youth, Paul would climb over the back wall in order to get in alone and wander round absorbing the atmosphere. He didn't have the Friends of Highgate Cemetery card I'd been issued with. Without this, or being one of a party of tourists, it's hard to get into the cemetery because of protracted vandalism to the catacombs and headstones. Even, it was alleged, black magic rituals had been carried out in the dead of night. Could he, in his wildest youthful dreams, have imagined he'd be lying in the damp earth of this place and never see old age, even middle age? The thought is too painful to bear.

We reach his grave. *I can't, I won't look.* Brownish remains of wreaths, discoloured ribbons. Fresh laurel spread all over. I looked. *OK! Now don't think. How can you stop thinking?*

'Shall we take some of this laurel and plant it in the garden? It might root.'

'Oh, yes – let's.'

The next grave has a cherub with a broken arm. There's the wall he must have climbed over. My heart is broken.

As we leave with our pathetic twigs of laurel, two of the 'friends' of Highgate cemetery, grim-faced elderly ladies, stop us. 'You're not allowed to take anything from the cemetery,' one says, her eyes out on stalks. The other nods in agreement. Their tactlessness is staggering. I can hardly speak. Heidi and Helmut look shocked. 'My son is in here,' I say, voice strangled by tears and rage, 'and I'm taking these from his grave to put in my garden to see if they'll grow.' They purse their lips disapprovingly. 'Don't you know what it's like to lose someone?' I hiss. Tourists look at me. The 'friends' just stare. *'Go to Hell!'* I think. When we got home I wished I'd said it rather than thought it.

Neither Vic nor I are couch potatoes but for some reason, in those early barren days, we got into the habit of sitting glued to the television whenever possible, and often into the early hours of the morning. We even bought video games and a television remote control, unthinkable in our former lives. We'd sit just staring at the dots on the screen whirling into a myriad vague shapes, mesmerised by them. Or we'd get Teletext on screen and scan it endlessly, often gazing at the same display for hours. The screen acted like a morphine injection, numbing and enabling. One evening, the 6th of December, Teletext went completely wrong with a black line drawn across the top of the screen. The whole display was distorted, and this distortion lasted an hour. The odd thing was that coherent words kept appearing in the jumble in various sections of the screen against a background of all other words being completely scrambled. 'Why me?' flicked on several times. Then in another section 'Wicked'. Then quickly came 'Close to' and 'Funne'.

One's natural tendency is to read something into everything in the sort of situation we found ourselves in, especially in the light of the significant things that had already happened: Paul's spirit return on his birthday; his visit to Frank; the return phone call from the answering machine to his father's phone; Mr. Lister the medium and his startlingly accurate evidence. We were very conscious of having to resist this trap, to stay sceptical, clear-headed and objective. And, indeed, this wasn't too difficult for either of us as our inclination was to be on the borderlines of belief, although with an open mind. But – 'Why me?', 'Close to', 'Funne' and 'Wicked'? Apart from the last, they were completely self-explanatory and 'wicked' was a word much used by Paul to describe something very enjoyable.

The following morning, in the early hours, Vic and I awoke simultaneously hearing coughing in the corridor outside our bedrooms and someone clearing their throat. Curiously enough we weren't petrified; perhaps because we weren't on our own in the house. There's strength in numbers. Gorbie the Siamese cat who usually slept in my room, mostly in my bed, had refused to come into the room on that particular evening and coincident with the coughing began to howl piteously, but still wouldn't come in. In the morning we compared notes. We had both heard exactly the same things. On the evening of that day, stationed in front of the television again staring at Teletext, Channel 4 went wrong and the words 'The Big One' flashed on for a second. We both saw it and reacted in the same way – with amazement. Paul used this phrase continually. It was a major part of his vocabulary. On the eighth of December, glued to Teletext by this time, 'Widge' came up on screen twice as a substitute for 'Bridge'. 'Widge' was Paul's nickname. What was happening? Was Paul trying to speak to us, to reassure us, via the television? That's what it looked like.

The builders' days were numbered. It was obvious they were spinning things out and funds were getting dangerously low. Things came to a head when I returned to the house after shopping one day and saw blue-grey cigarette smoke curling round the plastic at the end of the back extension leading to the garden. Mick the plasterer had been smoking when I went out (tea break) and here he was, one hour later, still smoking. It wouldn't have been so bad if he'd got to the house at 8.30 in the morning, but he generally arrived closer to 9.30 and then put the kettle on. However, he always made sure he knocked off on the dot of 4 pm and I felt I was getting the short straw all the time. The others were turning up if and when they felt like it, or needed some cash. Young Ted had already asked me for a loan – 'advance wages' as he put it. I refused, much to his chagrin. There was Mick – a pink man. He was covered from head to foot in more Carlite Bonding than he'd ever managed to apply to the walls and ceilings, and sitting on an upturned bucket, smoking. I just looked at him. I've often been told my looks speak volumes. He slowly got to his feet, protesting: 'The others said they'd be here to help me, I've got to go to hospital with this eye infection.' I thought grimly, 'If only Paul was here, you'd have a black eye to go with the infection,' but said nothing. That evening I paid them all off and shut the door on them with a feeling of huge relief coupled with sheer panic at the amount of work still left to do in the house. It was just the two of us now.

Christmas 1992. Not a lot to feel cheery about, nonetheless I dug the decorations out of the shed and put them up. I wrapped tinsel round the standard lamp in lieu of a tree and strung the coloured lights round the sitting room. It all looked rather garish against a background of lurid yellow and tan wallpaper I'd yet to strip off. In the end, I didn't strip it but just painted over it. It was impossible not to think of last Christmas at Crowsley. That feeling of security in the bosom of your family is such an illusion. We are all on a knife's edge of life. How easy it is to slip and be chopped up into little pieces.

I had built up a small mountain of coloured candles which I couldn't stop buying ever since the funeral. Each evening we lit one for Paul. I kept the main supply of candles in an upstairs room, one the builders hadn't touched. It contained various pieces of furniture, some bedding, pictures and other odds and ends. A few days previously I'd taken some small ornaments – average height four to five inches – out of a box and arranged them, upright, on top of a small chest of drawers. When I went into the room to fetch more candles, I noticed that two blankets had been draped over the chest and the ornaments in such a way that the ornaments were still standing upright underneath. Also the blankets were folded into each other at the top of the drape in a kind of french pleat. Impossible to do this without knocking the ornaments down underneath. The weight of the blankets would have pulled them over. And what an intricate way to fix two blankets together, and why? This curious cover-up remained a mystery. I didn't do it, neither did Vic, even had we been able, and there was no-one else around.

We decided to get out of the house on Christmas Day so arranged with a friend, Noel (the one who'd told us about the medium), to go to him, taking the cooked turkey and all the trimmings. He lived alone in Camden Town, not too far away. Paul had 'emigrated' to Sri Lanka at the age of twenty-three. He emigrated to his grandparents' house (on his father's side) in Wigan in the north of England at the age of nine, and to the USA at the age of nineteen; and as he had returned within a fairly short time from both locations having got bored with foreign lands, the expectation was the Sri Lanka emigration would be more a protracted working holiday than anything else. Noel, who was born in the capital, Colombo, was in the country at that time. We'd been friends for many years in London and he kept a fatherly eye on Paul, who unsurprisingly decided after a relatively short while that the tropical island was not for him. 'Apart from the humidity and flies,' he wrote in a letter home, 'there are too many beggars without legs propelling themselves around the streets on home-made skateboards. You feel a tug at the hem of your jacket, look down, and it's one of these poor wretched people gazing up at you with their hand out.' The whole rather seedy atmosphere was impoverishing him spiritually and financially. Paul was never one to pass an unfortunate person by without emptying his – generally already fairly empty – pockets for them.

After Christmas dinner, Noel told us some of the results of Paul's three-month stay in Sri Lanka. I'm glad I never knew anything about it at the time. He was apparently incarcerated in Colombo for a week for knocking someone out in a bar during an argument about politics which developed into a fight. Unfortunately the 'someone' was the off-duty Chief of Police, who also happened to be Noel's cousin. What led to him being tied to a railway track, and not an unused one at that, Noel didn't know, nor how he managed to escape before the hourly train arrived. I shuddered to think of what might have been, even at that early stage of his chequered career. We could have lost him then. The tale of the railway line created a visual image for me of the 1920's silent film often shown in Hollywood biopics – *The Perils of Pauline*. A blonde vamp is tied to a railway line with the train approaching fast and only seconds to spare as she manages to throw off her bonds Houdini-like and fling herself to the side of the track. Not much needed changing to make it *The Perils of Paul*. To think he had survived these self inflicted dangers, even that long ago, was a kind of oblique comfort.

Noel is overly fond of whisky and what with the heat and the food, when I returned to the sitting room after doing the washing up, Vic was watching television and Noel was fast asleep. It seemed a shame to wake him, and we probably wouldn't have got much sense out of him if we did, so we left a note and went home with a great sense of relief that Christmas was over. I had to agree with the Queen that 1992 had been an 'annus horribilis'.

When I was a journalist on *The Sunday Times* in the late 1970s my great friend and mentor was fellow journalist Jack Hallam. He was the picture editor on the paper. In his spare time he wrote ghost books, or rather collected and edited other people's ghost stories. I helped him with his research and sometimes went with him to haunted locations. The Theatre Royal, Drury Lane was one, haunted by 'The Man in Grey', a tall, upright young man, dressed in eighteenth century clothing – a tricorn hat and long grey cloak. The hilt of a sword can be seen protruding from his cloak. He had been reported for well over a century, taking a walk from one end of the balcony to the other, often during rehearsals for what generally proved to be a 'hit' production. He was seen from the stage by all the cast of the musical *The King and I* – a huge success – as well as by performers in other successful musicals in the years after the last war. Jack, some other people and I once sat in the darkened auditorium, a dim light from the wings half illuminating the stage, as we waited for the 'Man in Grey' to materialise. Nothing happened. Jack believed in ghosts because when he was a child he had seen his own mother appear at the foot of his bed at the moment she died in hospital several miles away.

Twenty years later I still hadn't seen a ghost, but in the last four months, I had witnessed and heard certain things which made me wonder about everything. It does seem inconceivable, when looking up at the vastness and beauty of the sky, trying to grasp the boundlessness of space, that this is it - our short span and then oblivion! And if all energy is matter and matter cannot die, then we cannot die, but are simply transmuted into another form of energy. We push up the daisies and enrich the earth which then feeds more of humankind. But what about the spirit? A tree is the same molecular construction as ourselves and a chair – and a parking meter. But they don't have spirits! As I gaze up from the garden at my bedroom on the top floor of the back extension on one of those last days in the last week of 1992, smoke from the fire ebbing and flowing before it, I see Paul in my mind's eye standing at the open window last summer looking out at me. I am balanced on the mound of rubbish left by the previous owners, marvelling at how people could live like this in such squalor, projecting my mind forward to getting rid of it all, seeing how the garden will look eventually – a raised rockery at the end, brick paved patio, my stone cherub holding a bird bath. Paul is laying new floorboards in my bedroom as last night one of the legs of my bed ruptured a whole corner section of them, full of dry rot. The day is bright and hot. Birds twitter on the waste ground at the rear. All around is the noise of London,that subdued roar of traffic, people, animals, machinery, electricity – the eternal background to everyone's lives in this great city. There is a feeling of excitement. There is always a crackling in the air when Paul is around. He leans on the cill and shouts something to me. I can't hear him properly. I peer at the window now through the eddying smoke of the dying fire. There's no-one there. Grimy cracked panes of glass set in decaying wood stare blankly back.

The search

Wood Green Spiritualist Church, due north from the City, is in a side street off one of those endless arteries bounded by 1930s ribbon development which intersect suburban London. It pulsates with traffic and walking there, a distance of about five miles, means breathing in more car exhaust fumes than oxygen. But Vic and I like walking, apart from which you could wait for ever for a bus and we had no car. It was mid-February 1993 and this was our first visit to a Spiritualist Church. Although we hadn't expressed the thought, both of us were expecting to see a proper church, with a steeple. What we found was a one-storey structure built from concrete blocks standing in a tarmac yard. A blue neon cross was fixed to the outside of the building. The front door was open and some people were trickling in and milling around. A middle-aged man in a brown suit stood in the entrance lobby. There were books and pamphlets laid out on trestle tables on either side and a saucer with a few coins in it. Not sure of what to give, we put two one pound coins in the saucer and the man gave us a hymn book each.

We drifted into the hall with the other people. Wooden pews arranged in rows; vases of flowers; a familiar picture of worn hands clasped, apparently in prayer – a stage with a piano, and a lectern. A wooden board with hymn numbers slotted into it hung to the right. A few people sitting in small huddled groups well to the back looked up rather suspiciously as we chose our places. We sat as far back as possible too. There was a curious mixture of expectancy and depression in the air. The door leading into the hall was heavy, lined with some sort of black rubbery material and studded like those in old cinemas with the 'Exit' sign above, dimly lit behind cracked yellowing glass. Each time it closed behind someone it made a dull thud, when all heads would turn to look at the newcomer and every eye would follow him or her to their seat. It was quite unnerving.

There was a final thud of the door and the man in the brown suit walked up the aisle importantly and climbed the steps to the stage. He leaned heavily on the lectern and began to talk. What he said couldn't have been very interesting as afterwards we didn't remember a word of it. Then everyone stood up, so we did as well, and sang a hymn. We all sat down. The man resumed his place at the lectern. He talked some more, something to do with a collection held the week before and how much had been raised. There was a little buzz of conversation, the man held up his hand with gravitas to silence it. Then he announced: 'And now, to take the platform for a demonstration of clairvoyance – Miss Ida Stenning, the president of our church.' He extended his hand to the wings with a flourish and backed off, leading a flurry of clapping.

A frisson of excitement ran through the congregation. People straightened in their seats and moved slightly so as not to be directly behind someone in front. There was a pregnant pause, then the president entered stage-left on stiletto heels and teetered across. The lectern arrested her flight and she anchored herself to it, beads swaying. I have never actually seen Noël Coward's play *Blithe Spirit* but Miss Stenning was what I imagine the medium in the play, Madame Arcati, looks like. A wafer-thin scrap of a woman of indeterminate age, but not under sixty-five. She had bluish-grey hair in curls, and a lot of make-up most of which had slightly missed the mark, especially the lipstick. As well as the beads – three rows of glass and amber – she wore dangling diamante earrings, bangles, several chiffon scarves, one wound round her head, another floating from her wrist, a diaphanous dress with an uneven hem, and false teeth. That the teeth were false was obvious because as she spoke, eyes closed and head tilted back, they kept falling from her upper jaw, rather muffling her words.

She seemed to speak for hours. It was hard to follow what she said. I think it was a kind of pep talk full of homilies and parables and personal anecdotes about her spiritual passage through life's troubled waters but it didn't quite hang together and her voice kept going up and down in the wrong places. The congregation, if we could call ourselves that, began to fidget. Madame Arcati took no notice. She carried on with her address, eyes closed, hands devoutly folded. It was hard to tell if she was even aware anyone else was there. It was obvious everyone was waiting for the 'messages' from the other side to begin and equally obvious she wasn't going to give them until she'd exhausted her repertoire. Finally she finished, delicately adjusted her bangles and her false teeth and began:

'I have a message for the lady in the blue coat in the middle over there. Yes, you my dear.' She waggled her finger in mild irritation. The lucky recipient squirmed in her seat and looked faintly embarrassed, even from the back. 'I have a father figure here for you dear, or it could be a grandfatherly figure.' *How's that for hedging your bets?* I thought. 'He gives you a red rose. Can you accept that dear?' The woman nodded. 'Speak up please dear, so everyone can hear you.' The woman shifted in her seat again. 'Ah, yes. He's coming to me very strongly now. Can you accept the name Tom or Thomas or Tony? Someone on your mother's side. Does Mary mean anything to you? Yes, I see her now, a lady who suffered with her legs on this side of life. She passed with a heart condition. She says to tell you she's free of pain now. All the pain has left her. She's very close to you. You've had a very difficult time these last few months, but things will get better. She's fading now, she's gone.' The woman nods assent. 'Take that with you, will you dear?'

Vic and I look at each other. This was pretty unspecific stuff and 'Take that with you, dear' seemed to be a catch phrase in the mediumship profession. Madame Arcati moved on to someone else. It was all fairly uninspiring as it was impossible to know whether what she said to people, the messages she gave, meant anything to them or not. They all looked so blank. They might as well have been standing in a queue at the supermarket. What had they come for? There was no feedback. 'I'm coming to the gentleman at the back sitting next to the blonde lady.' I looked up and down the back pews to see who she meant. 'You dear, you!' she exclaimed, pointing in our direction. *'Oh, God. It's Vic!'* I hastily switched on my small tape recorder. I wasn't going to rely on my memory this time. Vic motioned towards himself, mouthed 'Me?' and blushed, looking like he wanted the ground to open up. He doesn't like being the focus of attention. Everyone in front turned round to look at him.

'A lady in her seventies,' Madame Arcati had already launched into her message, 'with a lot of curly grey hair, well built. She's got her arm on your shoulders. She had a very difficult life, very hard-working woman. She's got a man with her. He passed over very suddenly, quite recently. You're not new to this. You're psychic yourself or have seen other mediums. I see a lot of sadness, tears. But the New Year is very good. A new beginning. You've left something behind.'

She didn't say, 'Will you take that with you, dear?' It was almost as though she'd heard our unspoken scornful thought. We were so staggered she'd come to us with a message we couldn't concentrate on what she went on to say to anyone else. When we got home and played the tape back we had to agree that the little she'd told us had been essentially correct. The lady in her seventies would be my mother. She was seventy-three when she died. She did have a lot of curly grey hair and she was extremely fond of Vic, her youngest grand-child, and would probably have had her arm round him. She did have a hard life, partly because she married a widower with six children and then had six of her own, I being the last of the line. The man she had with her who passed suddenly quite recently must be Paul. The bit about 'not being new to this' and being 'psychic yourself' was a generalisation which could be applied to anyone, but in fact, Vic had had psychic experiences from childhood. Mention of having seen other mediums. true, but only one other so far. The statement about 'sadness, tears and the New Year being a new beginning' was another generalisation, but then again, very relevant.

We had to decide whether the wheat outweighed the chaff. On balance, we thought it did. We, or rather I, revised my opinion of Ida Stenning. We were newcomers to the church, she had no inkling of who we were or our back-ground. If she was a charlatan she could easily have ignored us and concentrated on the regulars from whom she might have picked up some information in the past . But she went for the jugular and impressed us both. The evening's events gave us some more food for thought.

I was now beginning to be able to go out without crying over everybody. But if I met anyone who had known Paul it was a real struggle to stop the tears from surfacing. I took to wearing dark glasses. One day in the newsagents (minus glasses or I probably wouldn't have spotted it) I noticed a newspaper named *Psychic News*. I bought it. I found it interesting reading and especially noted a small piece about a woman who had seen a medium in Chesterfield, Derbyshire named Rita Rogers. This lady had given the woman remarkable evidence that her daughter still lived on in the spirit world. Rita Rogers apparently specialised in helping parents who had lost children. I made a mental note to go and see her some time. A coupon in the middle of the paper advertised a new journal, *Psychic World*, first issue out in March. I filled it in and sent if off. Various spiritualist churches were listed towards the back and running my eyes down this section, they lighted on Edmonton Church. Under this heading I read: 'Psychic Development Circle: Tuesday evenings 8 to 10'.

Tuesday evening two weeks later, the circle was enlarged by one. There were eight others, four women and four men, so my presence rather unbal-anced it. The leader was Shirley. She had frizzy brown hair and I'm sure she was a school-teacher during the day though she never said. A lot of the circle time was spent in listening to her reading out lists of people to send absent healing thoughts to, most of whom appeared to be her relatives. 'And those poor suffering children in Bosnia' was usually tacked on the end of her list.

Sometimes we did psychometry. This means each person putting a personal item like a ring or a watch into a tray with eyes closed, and taking an item off the tray afterwards – with eyes open, so you don't pick your own thing up. You then hold the item you picked up and try to get information from it – whose it is, what its associations have been. This can then be verified (or otherwise) by its owner at the end. This exercise is quite interesting and appears to have a certain amount of validity.

Then there was visualisation (imagining you're somewhere other than in a dingy, draughty room in a scruffy part of north-east London). We also did candle meditation. A lit candle is placed in a saucer on the floor in the middle of the circle. Shirley always led this by declaiming in a slow meaningful tone: 'Take the light into your head, down into your chest, through your arms,' — and she droned on until the whole of one's anatomy had been covered finishing up at the feet where 'the light drains away through them taking all evil with it.' This was virtually impossible to do. I never succeeded. The candle flame flickered hypnotically and I just drifted off.

Returning home in the evening after the circle, the journey became so hazardous with yobs, drunks, punks, drug-addicts and just plain nasty people looking for trouble on and off the bus, that I gave up the circle after a few weeks. I didn't miss it much.

The weather started to get better. Green shoots appeared in the garden, amazed to be able to see light after years of being buried under the mound. An old buddleia rooted in the brick wall at the back had room to wave its new branches around. Even the purple irises rescued from under a collapsed wall in front of the house pushed their stiff dark green points through the surprisingly rich soil and looked as though they might flower. I found a climbing rose named 'Paul's Scarlet' and planted it next to the shed with another rose a hybrid tea 'Deep Secret'. The label promised it would be a dark velvety red. It was a beginning. The next job was to be the patio, paved with the old bricks that were stacked up in the corner.

At the end of March the first issue of *Psychic World* arrived. Glancing through I noticed: Editor: Simon Forsyth; Features Editor: Alan Crossley. Crossley is a family name on my mother's side and suddenly seemed significant, especially as Paul's flat had been in Crossley Street too. On impulse, I wrote a letter to Mr. Crossley mentioning the loss of my eldest son, my background as a journalist, and the surname connection between us. He must have been surprised to receive my letter, out-of-the-blue, as I didn't hear from him. Some weeks later the phone rang. It was a man who introduced himself as Simon Forsyth, editor of *Psychic World*.

'Alan Crossley sent me your letter,' he said. 'Will you write for us?'

Without a moment's hesitation I replied 'Yes!'

'Let's meet,' he said.

A week later, at 2 pm I'm sitting in a café in High Holborn, Central London looking at every man who pauses outside the underground station opposite. It would have been sensible to have asked Mr. Forsyth a few more questions about his appearance, or if he'd strike the classic pose with a rolled up copy of *The Times* in his left hand and a carnation in his buttonhole. There seem to be an awful lot of men with dark hair aged about 30 wearing suits hanging around outside the station.

Suddenly, I see him. I rush out of the café and across the road losing sight of him momentarily behind swirling buses, cars and lorries.

'It's you, isn't it?' I say, reaching the safety of the other side.

'Yes' he replies 'Judith?'.

'Yes.'

'Fine. Let's go across to that café and have a cup of coffee.'

We thread our way back through the thundering traffic and sit down at the table I've just vacated.

Half an hour later I'm not on the payroll of *Psychic World* because the paper can't afford to pay anyone. Simon is a postman from Manchester who decided one day to start up a psychic newspaper by borrowing £3,000. When I probe him to find out why, as setting up a newspaper, even a monthly, is quite a big undertaking, especially for someone who hasn't been in the profession, his laconic answer is: 'I went into the library and picked up a psychic book and that started me thinking.' I ask him what sort of stuff he'd like me to write and he shrugs and says: 'Whatever you like. I'm sure you know. Why don't you ring up Michael Roll. He'll give you Gwen Byrne's number. Here's his number. I'd better go now, I've got to get back up to Manchester, I'm on the night shift. Oh, and by the way, you can be the Assistant Editor.'

And that was that. From redundant building site foreman to unpaid assistant editor in one short step. Things were looking up. I rang up Michael Roll. He was in Bristol. He sounded pleasant and under pressure. He said he'd send me some literature. When the envelope arrived I ripped it open. Two photocopied articles tumbled out. 'The Greatest Love Story Ever Told' and 'Physically Meeting "Dead" People Completely Changed My Life' by Michael Roll'.

I had to read the one about 'meeting "dead" people' first. It was about Mr. Roll's belief that we all survive physical death and how lucky he was having been born the son of a rationalist mother who made a careful study of the work of Arthur Findlay and Sir William Crookes (I had yet to discover who these two gentlemen were). This study by Mr. Roll's mother had enabled him to bypass the psychic jungle; a sort of minefield – as he described it – laid to trap those who make an effort to find out whether we survive death or not. Later in the article, he mentioned having been lucky enough to witness an incredible experiment in materialisation (this I later learned is when a medium can apparently summon up a dead person to re-appear in the form they had in life). The medium whose experiment Mr. Roll was present at was a lady named Rita Goold and, I read, Mr. Roll had been re-united with his 'dead' father, and Mr. Alan Crossley, who was also present, with his 'dead' wife. Now I knew a little bit more about Alan Crossley, the Features Editor of *Psychic World*. All I'd read was mind-blowing stuff, but was it true?

The other article was about Russell Byrne... Byrne? the name rang a bell. He had died of cancer in 1963 at the age of nine and had 'materialised' in the 1980s to ask if he could be reunited with his mother and father. He supplied their address and telephone number to the medium Rita Goold to whom he materialised. This was even more over-the-top than the first article. I wasn't mentally prepared to take all this on board. I had to meet the mother and father of this little boy and try and make a judgment for myself. My mind clicked back to Simon. He had mentioned Gwen Byrne. She would be the mother. I must go and see her. I picked up the torn envelope. Out of it fluttered a little piece of paper. 'Pink Panther Society' was written on it, and 'Gwen Byrne'. Underneath was her telephone number in Essex.

I went to Rayleigh in Essex by train on a bright sunny day in May. Gwen had agreed to give me an interview for the paper and it was a chance to hear her and her husband Alfie's story first-hand. They live in a pleasant suburban area and as I walked up to the front door it was hard to reconcile this unpretentious house in an ordinary street with the extraordinary events they claim to have witnessed: the materialisation of their young son Russell who had been dead for over twenty years.

Gwen is what is generally described as a 'glamorous gran'. Black bouffant hair, liberal make-up, young clothes. Alfie clearly adores her. They gave me an unreserved welcome and we all sat down with a cup of tea and began to talk as though we'd known each other for years. In essence, this is what they told me:

Russell had died aged nearly ten from cancer. Gwen described her feelings at the time as being 'close to going completely insane with grief'. She spent some time in hospital with a nervous breakdown. After many months had passed both she and Alfie began to search for Russell. Over the course of years, they visited mediums and were given what they considered a great deal of evidence of life after death. One evening in the mid-1980s they received a phone call from a man who had been present at a seance conducted by the medium Rita Goold in Leicester. The man said he had been given their address and phone number by their son Russell who had materialised at the seance. Gwen and Alfie rushed over to Rita Goold's house at the first oppor-tunity, and during the next two to three years, on numerous occasions during séances with her, they saw Russell materialise in the form he had the last time they saw him alive as a small boy. They touched him, he felt warm. He spoke to them, they recognised his voice; he sat on their knees, played with objects in the room, even gave them gifts and convinced them they were seeing, hearing and touching their 'dead' son.

I asked if they paid to attend these séances and they replied they didn't. Were they still going to them? They said Rita Goold had stopped them because she had received intimidating and threatening phone calls. They didn't know from whom or why.

To accept an account such as the one I was given by Gwen and Alfie Byrne requires a great leap of faith. Despite the intimations of immortality I had already experienced in a small way, I wasn't able to take the leap at that stage. I hoped with all my heart it was true and wished that Mrs. Goold was still holding séances and I could visit her and perhaps see Paul. But my over-whelming feeling was one of qualified scepticism.

They asked if I knew of the Lynwood Foundation. I said I didn't. They described it as a 'family' drawn from all over the British Isles, and abroad, who meet for residential spiritual and psychic weeks in various locations in England. The man running it was a spiritualist medium named Don Galloway. The next week organised would be in Castleton, Derbyshire. Gwen said some of her mums in The Pink Panther Society would be there. She said Russell had given her a toy pink panther and asked her, during one of his materialisations, to set up a society for bereaved mothers in order that they could contact and comfort each other and exchange experiences. 'We're going to Castleton for a week at the end of August; would you like to come?' Gwen asked. I thought, maybe I would. The next day I wrote a piece for the paper about Gwen and Alfie and their alleged miracle.

Vic joined a Band. He played saxophone and had been reading *Melody Maker* for weeks looking for ads for a saxophonist. The group met in Ealing in West London and played Salsa and Caribbean music which wasn't exactly his taste – he preferred Blues and Jazz – but it was better than not playing at all. He'd also got a job, working for an agency. I was glad because he'd been spending too much time in the house and getting very introspective. After all my hard work cleaning his flat, his ex-fiancée had returned a few weeks later and moved back in with a new boyfriend. Vic naturally had immediately stopped his share of the mortgage repayments and there was now a wrangle going on between solicitors to sort out the mess. It wasn't very uplifting, so going out to work again and playing in a band would help take his mind off his misfortunes.

As I was now alone in the house a lot I could indulge my grief which was still near the surface. Only nine months had passed. A gestation period. Whether indulging grief was a good or bad thing I didn't know. The doctor whom I had to see frequently for supplies of Migraleve (I've always been plagued by migraine headaches) advised me to go to a bereavement counsellor. I refused. If Vic and I couldn't help each other I didn't see that an outsider could contribute anything. Being told 'time will heal' and 'you'll get over it' does absolutely nothing. It's like being told the Third World is starving, therefore you should be happy with your lot. There are no connections. Perhaps time will heal and you will get over it. But if at the time in question you are suffering, to hear that at some time in the future you may be healed is worse than useless. In fact, the one and only thing which was making my loss remotely bearable was the discovery there might be something more out there. That this, perhaps, wasn't it, and one day I might see Paul again. I made an appointment to see Rita Rogers, the medium I'd read about in *Psychic News* last winter. She was the one who specialised in helping bereaved parents. A man answered the phone. When I asked for a sitting, he riffled through a book (I heard the pages rustling) and said: 'She's very busy, but what about June 26th?'

'Fine,' I replied.

At Chesterfield Station I get a taxi to Lower Pilsey. 'Do you want Ash House?' the driver enquires.

'Yes,' I answer.

'Thought you did. There's a woman there tells fortunes.'

The house is quite large, set back off the road, hidden by high hedges. A troupe of garden gnomes assembled near the path to the front door is a bit daunting, but I press on (I've travelled three

Rita Rogers. Photo: Victor Chisholm.

hundred miles) and ring the bell. The door is opened by a dark-haired woman in a slightly faded blue dress and carpet slippers.

'I've an appointment with Rita Rogers,' I say.

'That's right love, come on in.' She ushers me into a dark hallway. 'Go in there love, sit yourself down. I won't be a minute.'

I find myself in a room full of brown panelling and horse brasses. They glitter from every inch of a huge fireplace surround. As I sink into a massive black vinyl sofa a rough voice screams: 'Sit yourself down! Sit yourself down! Who's a lovely boy?' It's a parrot! I look at the poor thing with a mixture of horror and pity – I hate to see birds in cages, especially large birds, and at the same time it suddenly dawns on me that the woman who opened the door *is* Rita Rogers. The parrot, head on one side, regards me sagely. Gnomes, horse brasses, a parrot! All my innate, generally suppressed, middle-class prejudices rise up. I'm almost at the point of getting up and going, encouraged by a glance at the cuckoo clock above the fireplace which tells me I've been waiting in this gloomy parlour for half an hour, when I hear a murmur of voices in the hallway. The previous client is leaving. The front door opens and closes, then the door of the room I am in opens, the parrot screeches, and before I know what's happened, I am in another room sitting on a low sofa in front of Rita Rogers.

We look at each other silently. Remembering Ida Stenning and Mr. Lister I tell myself to keep an open mind. I look around the room. The walls are covered with dozens of colour snapshots of children and babies. I guess these are some of the departed children whose mothers and fathers she's helped to comfort with messages from the other side of the veil. She continues to regard me speculatively. I feel extremely uncomfortable, and tearful, but I smother the tears and try to look sophisticated and controlled. I ask her if I can switch on the tape recorder I've brought with me. It's in my handbag. She says, 'No, I'd rather you didn't.' This makes me even more uneasy and I surreptitiously switch it on anyway by slipping my hand inside my bag and feeling for it. The bag is open at the top so I know my recorder has a good chance of picking up what's said. She begins to talk about her activities earlier in the day. I wonder why on earth she's telling me all this. She rambles on for around a quarter of an hour – about herself; about being from a Romany family. She tells me she's written a book, that she helps the police find missing children.

I really wish I hadn't come three hundred miles to hear all this and project myself forward to the sweet moment when I can leave, get to the station as fast as my legs can take me, and get back home. I'm just putting the kettle on at home when she asks: 'Who's Steven and who's John?'

I return to Ash House, Lower Pilsley with a jolt to hear her saying: 'I don't like this John. It's not so much what he did as the way that he did it. He's not a good person, he made you suffer. *He* doesn't like him much either. He's going somewhere I wouldn't like to go when he dies. He's got eighteen months, he's not a good person. If I'd known you when you met him I'd have said don't marry him.'

My jaw drops in astonishment. Steven is Paul's cousin. He was always at the forefront of Paul's mind. They spent a great deal of time together as children. In fact, he and his sister Siobhan left home and lived with us for months on end. John! Well, she had stated without equivocation who and what John was in relation to me. That he had only eighteen months to live was something that remained to be proved, although he wasn't in good health. To say I am surprised by what I hear is an understatement. But there is more. 'This man,' she says, 'the man who's speaking to me, says he's your brother. She is my sister, he says. He is full of love for you, full of you. He won't reveal your age. Is he your son?'

I have said nothing up to this point but here I answer 'Yes' in a weak sort of voice. Paul always told everyone I was his sister. I looked so young for so long he got fed up with explaining to his friends that I was his mother, and it cramped his style. So I became his sister. And I forbade him, later on, to tell anyone my age. In fact, I don't think he ever knew my age for certain. He never even bothered to remember his own. Now I am hanging on every word Rita is saying, hoping the little recorder in my bag is picking it up too. Memory is fallible.

'He passed in a building,' she's saying. 'There were other people there. He wasn't alone, there was a girl with him. She put something in his drink. He began to die in the club or the pub, with other people. She didn't mean to kill him. She was jealous, jealous of everyone. She just did it to keep him – make him more like her. She was obsessive. He told her it was the last night with her. She couldn't stand that. She has to live with that. She put on a good show of grieving didn't she? Were drugs involved?'

I nod dumbly.

'He wasn't a drug taker. He was experimenting. It all went tragically wrong. He died suddenly. Here one minute, gone the next. Young, and not long ago.'

My mind flashes back to Richard in the pub after the funeral. *'She put something in his drink,' isn't that what he said? 'She was jealous of him. 'Drugs; experimenting with them – it went tragically wrong, and he died suddenly. It was the last night with her.' Oh, God! Paul – why didn't you tell me? I would have got rid of her, locked and barred the door – anything, anything to stop this happening.* I feel a great upsurge of emotion but sternly stifle it. I must listen to every word.

'He's very angry. He doesn't want to be remembered to her.' Rita is speaking again. 'She will be charged with murder when she passes. She'll die of a drugs overdose, but she won't go where he is. He's on a very high plane; he's a beautiful person. He says, "Don't have anything to do with her. She's dangerous."'

I am completely overwhelmed by what I am hearing. Can this woman whom I've never seen in my life be telling me all this ?

'He knew he wouldn't live to be old,' she's continuing. 'He'd only have had another five years anyway.'

I ask her what is the name of the man who's speaking to her. She says 'P – Peter. No! – Peter is who took him over. It's Paul.'

I am speechless.

I leave Chesterfield with a lot of think about. Rita Rogers has given me information that she had no prior access to whatsoever. We had never met each other, she didn't even know my name or where I came from. I was a complete stranger. Yet she told me things about my life only someone who knew me could have told her. They were specific. Names were given, events described. How did she get this information? Sceptics would say: 'Super ESP'.

What does this really mean? It means the ability of a person to obtain information from another's mind. I would see this ability as another kind of miracle and I don't think I have ever read or witnessed a demonstration of this kind of power. If such people existed, anywhere in the world, I think we would all have heard about them. To put it in military terms, they would only have to meet the general to know his whole plan of attack. The war would be won. I don't deny the existence of telepathy; I have been an unwitting participant in the transmission or reception of telepathic messages many times. Telepathy comes from the conscious mind. But to be able to draw the kind of information Rita had given me from another's subconscious mind! That was a totally different arena. And if, after all, it was Super ESP, why wasn't she rich, in demand by governments, spy-masters, industrialists, drug enforcement agencies, crime-busters, gangsters to plunder the minds of all those with something to keep secret? And why, in my case, was all she said specifically related to Paul? My subconscious, like everyone else's, is full of billions of pieces of information. Why should she carefully draw out precise and detailed facts from it which linked with him? Was he there, speaking to her from the spirit world, wherever that is, using her as a medium to tell me what had happened, to confirm things other people had said, to give evidence that he was still alive in another dimension?

Three years after my sitting with Rita Rogers, Princess Diana flew with Dodi Fayed in the Harrods jet to have a sitting with her. A few short weeks later they were both dead. Her reading for me was so staggeringly accurate that I am sure Rita would have been told by spirit communicators of this impending disaster, but it seems that what will be, will be and there is such a thing as destiny. On the way back from Chesterfield to London this tragedy was in the future and I was preoccupied with trying to find my own answers. When I got home I had still come to no conclusion but my flame of hope was burning a little stronger.

That night I had a dream in which I knew the flame had died a little: I had been doubting all I had experienced and been told about the spirit world. In the dream, I entered an empty room. As I entered I was pulled by the wrist by an unseen force quite roughly, further into the room, towards some outside steps. As I was going down the steps, I was given another little shove, then I woke up. A few days later I received a letter from Heidi, our German friend in Ireland. She wrote that some days before, on the same night I'd dreamt of the empty room, she had a dream of Paul visiting them. She said he looked very happy and relaxed, exactly the way he looked the last time she saw him. He was wearing jeans and a jumper. This was a very spontaneous letter from Heidi as she doesn't believe in the supernatural and I had not mentioned any of the psychic 'happenings' which Vic and I had been involved in since Paul died. The two dreams seemed to be a slap on the wrist for me from another dimension.

The week with the Lynwood Spiritual Fellowship in Castleton proved to be the right time in the right place. It started on August 21st and ended on the 28th, thus encompassing the first anniversary of Paul's death which would otherwise have been a dismal day spent at home. Don Galloway – tall, precise but welcoming, founder of the Fellowship, had organised the seminar consummately, drawing on his long experience of such gatherings. It was, as Gwen had promised, like becoming the newest member of a large family.

Vic and I needed this kind of warm embrace. We were a truncated family by the time Paul was an adult. Both sets of grandparents dead; most of my brothers, sisters and their children scattered throughout the world and the ones who were in England, apart from my brother Gerald who came to Paul's funeral and his wife Ruth, were dismissive of Paul in particular and tended to sideline us as a unit.

The Victorian mansion, Losehill Hall, in a village appropriately named Hope, was filled with activity – talks, awareness groups, psychometry, numerology, healing, demonstrations of clairvoyance, philosophy, meditation. But the over-riding benefit, to me at any rate, was the knowledge that I wasn't alone in my search. Others were looking too, and some had found what they were looking for. The last evening of the week was for letting your hair down. It always amazes me what hidden talents people have. Someone told jokes – perhaps they'd told the same ones at many previous Lynwood gatherings, but they were new to us, and very funny. Everyone else seemed to enjoy them too. A husband and wife (he was something very important in international politics) did a double act. He played the piano, she danced, like a puppet on a string, all jerky and out of synch. That made their performance hilarious as I think it was meant to be soulful and we weren't supposed to laugh. Gwen Byrne sang. That was really a treat. She has the most wonderful soprano voice, high and vibrant, sweet and poignant. Alfie, her husband, looked on proudly. I could have listened to her for another week.

After the entertainment, Gwen grabbed my arm. 'You've got to meet one of the Pink Panther mums,' she said and steered me over to a slight, dark-eyed woman whom I hadn't seen before. She had come to Losehill Hall just for the day. 'This is Gill,' Gwen said. 'You two have got something in common.' Gill Smith had lost her adult son Stephen five years before. 'He was under a lot of stress,' she said, 'and took an overdose of drugs.' Gill and I talked for some time, in tune with each other's loss. 'Do you know Douglas Druce?' she asked. 'He lives in London. He has a circle. You should meet him.'

I didn't know it at the time but this short meeting with Gill and her mention of Douglas Druce was instrumental in setting me on the path of the most important discovery in my life.

James Thurber, an American humourist, wrote a chapter in one of his books headed 'The Night the Bed fell on Father'. The whole book was very funny, although I can't now remember its title, but this particular chapter struck me at the time I read it as being hilarious. The heading has always stuck in my mind – another one of those billions of inconsequential items which our subconscious stores away to gather dust. Saturday 4th September 1993 was the first anniversary of Paul's funeral. It was also the night the ceiling fell on mother. Not my mother, she died in 1969: it fell on Andrea's mother. This sounds heartless but I hasten to add, the ceiling – or part of it – fell round her rather than on her despite the fact she was sitting directly beneath it.

What happened was this: Mee Lin, Andrea's mother, was in a chair near the meagre fire in the sitting room. I was in that room too. Vic and Andrea were in the kitchen. It was a very cold evening and she, coming from Malaysia, feels the cold. I offered to fetch an electric fire for her and went upstairs to the room directly above the sitting room to find it. The room was packed with everything you could think of, and parts of the floorboards were up, exposing the joists beneath. Also, it was dark. The wiring hadn't been completed in that room, and the only light came from the street lamps outside. In my haste to find the electric fire, and because of the dark, I inadvertently stepped into one of the gaps in the floor There was an almighty bang. My whole leg disappeared into a gaping hole and I saw the huge ornate plaster rose from the ceiling below, heavy with acanthus leaves and fruit, hurtling downwards towards Mee Lin.

I thought I'd killed her, but I couldn't get my leg out of the hole, it was trapped at the thigh by the broken, rotten joists. Eventually I pulled it out and, in acute pain, flew downstairs and into the sitting room. It was as though a bomb had just exploded. The whole room was swirling with white plaster dust, chunks of ceiling rose were everywhere yet Mee Lin still sitting in the same chair in the same position as I'd left her, was untouched – just a bit of dust in her hair. I had to pretend I'd been in another part of the house and heard it happen. I couldn't admit I'd done it; if it hadn't been for the great cloud of plaster she would probably have seen my leg sticking out of the hole. I was so relieved she was all right that the pain in it disappeared – at least for the time being, while we were clearing up. It came back later. The leg hurt for weeks and a large section of it went blue, then yellow. Eventually all there was to show from the accident was a small indentation about an inch in diameter with no nerve endings. If one of those heavy pieces had hit Mee Lin she would have been injured without a doubt, perhaps even killed. I thanked whatever powers there are for preventing that from happening. I couldn't help thinking – perhaps it was Paul, stopping his mother from being a murderer.

Part of my schooldays were spent in Cliftonville, the better end of Margate in Kent. I say part, because according to my father my mother was a gypsy . No sooner had we settled in a house and they'd sorted out a school for me, than my mother would want to move again. I've inherited her itchy feet. When I saw a 'psychic weekend' advertised at The Royal Hotel, Clarendon Road, Margate, I had to go. I persuaded Andrea to come with me. She only agreed because she'd just passed her driving test and wanted to practise. That suited me fine. I hate driving.

Margate wasn't as I remembered it. It was never all that salubrious, but was it this grim? I looked round for familiar landmarks. Where was Dreamland, the fun-fair? Was the sandy beach full of little pools, seaweed and shells under the pier still the same? There was always a lovely scent at that spot, a mixture of vinegar, fresh air and seaweed. It didn't seem worth negotiating the greyness to go and see. It was November, but even so – was it really like this then? Clarendon Road I vaguely remembered – the name at least. The road itself could have been anywhere. It was desolate; full of mournfully empty hotels. Frayed striped awnings slapping in the wind; broken glass signs proclaiming grand names. We looked for somewhere to park the car. No room in the road, so we drove across the main esplanade towards the sea and parked in an almost deserted car park. We glanced meaningfully at each other. This was promising to be a disastrous weekend!

The Royal when we found it looked as grey and uninviting as the rest. A few hand-printed posters had been stuck up in windows advertising the event, the dull black-painted door was slightly ajar. We pushed it open and went in.

Inside reflected outside – uninviting! but not grey – more brownish. That was the overall impression. And a few lost looking people floating around. A girl stood behind a desk embellished with a quilted plastic fascia. She had a worried expression and a jumble of papers in front of her. She was chewing a plastic pen.

'Excuse me,' Andrea said. 'Can you tell us where our room is?'

The girl didn't respond, perhaps she was deaf. An older woman with blonde hair and a shiny exhausted face bustled up.

'Can I help you madam? And your booking is in the name of?' She smiled at us brightly and put her arm round the girl, squeezing her a mite too hard, 'They're my fledglings you know, they're just learning.' She leaned over the girl's shoulder. 'Your room's up on the fifth floor. I do hope you have a lovely stay with us this weekend, we have a very full programme.' Her smile seemed to be set in concrete.

Our room was no better and no worse than what we'd seen of the rest of the establishment. Yellowing venetian blinds hiked up at one side, and bulging, which wouldn't budge up or down, two single beds with wrinkled nylon sheets and a shower cubicle in the corner with basin. The basin had hairs in it. Whilst not expecting The Ritz this was probably worse accommodation than Holloway Jail. And that's free. We dumped our bags and got out of the room as quickly as possible.

On the ground floor a cut-out cardboard arrow pointed us in the direction of 'Refreshments', and underneath that was written 'Psychic Fayre'. I was all for getting a cup of tea but Andrea was waylaid by a girl sitting behind a table draped with a lopsided greenish cloth. The girl, who was wearing gypsy earrings and a scarf round her head, put her can of Coke down next to a transistor radio in the middle of some splayed out greasy Tarot Cards and said: 'Dje wan' yer forchune read?' Before I could catch Andrea's eye with a meaningful negative look, she'd dashed over and sat down in a chair in front of the girl, like a fish on a hook. So I had to sit on a black leatherette banquette which had seen better days and wait for her.

The main part of the 'Fayre' was in a large room and consisted of trestle tables with items on them like joss sticks and 'mood music' cassettes, silver jewellery – all that sort of thing. I managed to steer Andrea through this, without her buying anything, into the refreshment area. It was packed. Everybody who had booked for the weekend was in there eating and drinking madly. Trays were heaped, steam was rising. It was as if they had all just come off hunger strike. The evening's programme was in a cavernous, dingy below-street-level room with high barred windows. We sat in plastic chairs arranged in rows waiting for something to happen. Several people trooped in one behind the other and lined up in front of us. One of them was the blonde lady with the shiny face who'd spoken to us in the entrance hall. The girl who'd been behind the reception desk was there and several others dressed like her in a grey skirt and white blouse – awkward looking, rather like overgrown schoolgirls.

The blonde lady was obviously in charge. Her smile was still in place and she looked even more exhausted. 'Well, isn't this marvellous?' she said in a stagey voice. 'Welcome all of you – all you old faces, and some new ones' (coyly, in our general direction): 'we have a very full programme for you, but this evening I want you to meet our mediums. But first, for all of those who don't know me and' (skittishly) 'there's not many of those is there?' Faint laughter rippled through the audience. 'I'm Fiona Surtees, your organiser and master – or should I say mistress? – of ceremonies.' Her aside got a dutiful titter. 'And this,' laying her hand on the arm of a nice looking man standing next to her, 'is my husband, Keith. He is an international clairvoyant, medium and healer.' Keith looked slightly embarrassed. 'These' (Fiona indicated the schoolgirls) 'these are my fledglings, my trainee mediums. If you would like them to spread their wings with you, you'll find they don't charge as much as fully fledged mediums, naturally, and that's the way they'll learn.'

Andrea and I looked at each other. What had we got ourselves into? One of the men in the line-up standing next to a woman with jet-black hair, a red dress and white high-heeled sandals, took out a handkerchief and blew his nose loudly. Fiona responded to the signal. 'And this gentleman is the famous international medium Clive Philpott, as I'm sure you will all know, and we are lucky enough to have with us (turning to the lady in red) 'the internationally known clairvoyant and healer Myra Street from London.' The two acknowledged a flurry of clapping from the plastic chairs. 'Now we will have a short demonstration of clairvoyance and I will ask Clive to take it.'

Clive stepped forward as the others trooped off to sit down. He clasped his hands and closed his eyes. Everyone looked at him expectantly. He opened his eyes, focused them at an indeterminate spot in the middle distance above everybody's heads, and proceeded to give 'messages' to various people which were received in the low-key way I'd come to be familiar with. It was impossible to be sure if the recipients genuinely unknown to the medium were being

given relevant information (or irrelevant information as the case may be) or
if they were old-timers, or stooges, or even if they'd heard what he was saying.
For people who were allegedly receiving messages from the dead, the
response was so muted as to make one wonder which side of the veil the dead
were on. Or was it just English reserve? At 9.30 we escaped to our freezing
room on the fifth floor.

The next morning we ate our left-over sandwiches for breakfast and went
out for a cup of coffee. I'm sure the sea-front snack bar – the only one open
– was the same place where I'd helped out in my school holidays making the
latest food craze, dunkin' ring donuts, American style. We used to cook them
in deep oil, smother them with caster sugar, and stack them up on spikes.
They cost sixpence each. They were very popular, with a cup of frothy
espresso coffee. I could have eaten one there and then. The rest of the day we
stayed out, driving round.

Keith Surtees saved the weekend from being completely forgettable. I only
decided to have a sitting with him because he was nice looking. He led me to
one of the unused rooms. I sat on the bed, he on a facing chair. At first what
he said was fairly general: 'A fatherly vibration – dad or grandad; a lot of love
coming through; you've been on a very low mental and emotional plane,' and
so on. Then he said: 'I've got two people here, and a lady who is a bit shy and
reserved, coming in with the gentleman who I feel to be your father. She's
giving me the name of Maud.' That made me sit up, because my mother's
name *was* Maud. How on earth did he know that? Then there were some
more generalities which led to him saying something about 'breathing and a
strain on the heart due to a lung condition' and that someone was 'very close
who had suffered this type of condition.'

Then he said 'Paul-ine.' My heart skipped a beat. 'A feeling of a family situation. I'm getting a feeling of great loss and brightness, as if they weren't
expecting to go to spirit. I get liveliness, wonderful vibration and energy …
dancing, dancing. They might not be as young as they feel – about eighteen.'

How unexpected! Keith had produced two names – one, my mother Maud
(how could he pull that out of the hat and get it right?); he had correctly asso-
ciated her with my father, and Paul had changed into Pauline, to whom he
had linked 'a strain on the heart due to a lung condition' which was clinically
what caused Paul's death. He had also picked up on Paul's energy and liveliness and on the Peter Pan age factor and the 'family situation'. But why had
he changed Paul to Pauline? I was to discover a possible answer to this later

when I learned that spirits do not necessarily keep the same sex.

It could have been because it was a dank, depressing November in London or because it was one of the last things Paul said ('Shall I go to Ireland and start building that house?') but suddenly the idea of building on the four acres of mountain land we'd kept fallow for ten years seemed a good idea. Vic had inherited the land when Paul died as it was in their joint names, and it had planning permission which was about to expire. As the land was in a beauty spot on the west coast, about to become a heritage area, they probably wouldn't renew it. Helmut recommended a builder and said he'd supervise the initial construction of a one-storey simple house reflecting Irish traditional style. I refused to let anyone call it a bungalow as this horrible word conjures images of plastic-framed picture windows, York stone fascias, Austrian blinds and coach lamps. The house wasn't going to have any of *that*.

The first shock was a request from the builder for an extra £2,750 on his estimate to make a driveway to the site which sloped fifty feet from the road. I had nurtured a pleasant idea of a gently winding track smoothed out of the hillside, edged by shady trees and wild rhododendrons. The reality was a super highway in order to take concrete mixers, builders' supply lorries and earth gouging machinery down. And the second reality was they had to knock down all the trees and rhododendrons in that area to build it. After the house foundations were laid, work had to stop for three months while the rain poured down. Then it snowed, unusual for the west coast. Helmut sent us a photograph of a building site with an oblong of brickwork up to one level on it, and the majestic Caha mountains in the background crowned in white. I'd forgotten how beautiful they were.

The house in London was still needing crisis management. Vic had done a marvellous job in creating a fully tiled shower room where the builders' pallet had stood, with a tongue and groove boarded ceiling, and we'd got some kitchen units from Ikea, but we hadn't even touched upstairs. I sometimes wondered if we were doing the right thing getting involved in another house at the same time, but it was a now or never situation. Paul would have done it, we were following in his footsteps.

One day towards the end of November, while I was alone in the house painting over the yellow and tan wallpaper in the sitting room, I thought of Douglas. He was the man in Hampstead that Gill, whom I'd met at the Lynwood Fellowship, had told me about. He had his own psychic circle. I felt low again on that particular day, utterly depressed and lonely. There was a huge emptiness. I projected myself forward mentally to the rest of my life. It would all have to be lived without Paul. It was unbelievable he was no more. Every fibre ached for him to walk through the front door again with his swagger trying to hide his sensitivity, and failing. *Man that is born of woman hath only a short time to live*. I remembered the funeral service. How true that is. *But why, God, why? It should have been me, not him, in the natural order of things*. God didn't answer me. I picked up the phone and rang Douglas's number. I didn't have high hopes of anything coming of my call, but nothing ventured nothing gained! A very pleasant voice answered the phone. It was Douglas. I explained why I was ringing and asked if I could meet him one evening.

'Of course you can,' he said.

'Can I bring my son?'

'Be delighted to meet you both,' was his reply.

We fixed up a date. I felt a lot better after that call.

The Electronic Voice Phenomenon

We emerged from the underground station at about seven in the evening. It was just after Christmas, cold and wet. People, heads bent deep into collars, hurried home. Pavements glistened. We crossed the main road at traffic lights and saw Douglas Druce's street straight ahead. A yellow street lamp shone through a tracery of raindrops on a leafless tree making them sparkle like jewels. Belsize Park, Hampstead is one of those formerly upmarket areas of London which have been invaded by the itinerant population of the world, transforming the former one-family gentlemen's residences into dozens of one-person bed-sits. There seemed to be a large number of dogs in the neighbourhood judging by the state of the pavements, and it looked impossible to find a space to park a car. But that didn't bother Vic and me.

I felt a little nervous, standing on the step of Douglas' home – an Edwardian 4-storey house nearly at the end of a long narrow street. Vic rang the bell and we waited. 'Hello,' echoed from deep inside, then a clatter of footsteps. The door was flung wide open, light streamed out. 'Vic and Judith? – Come in, come in. I'm really glad to see you. Come upstairs.'

Douglas didn't look as I expected him to. From his voice on the phone, I thought he would be taller, thinner, older. He was compactly built, puckishly middle-aged, with a neatly trimmed beard and moustache. His face wore a huge smile and he radiated friendliness and warmth. We followed him through the hallway dividing door and up the stairs into his flat, and gasped. It was like entering fairyland. The banisters were wound with Christmas decorations: ribbons and glittering baubles; gold and silver plaited baskets of frosted shining fruit, white angels and huge shimmering butterflies perched on newel posts; glossy green leaves hung with deep red cherries plaited through the stair-rods; a suit of armour straight from Henry V standing on the landing. The helmet and visor were topped by a golden crown at a rakish angle. We glimpsed an enormous Christmas tree decorated with pink roses, ribbons and lights in a mirrored room. It was magical, like being a child again and thrilling to gossamer wings and stardust at your first pantomime.

'This is wonderful,' I said.

Douglas' grin grew wider. 'Come and meet the others.' We went into a kitchen that appeared to be papered with Christmas cards and full of people. He introduced us to them – Debbie, Maggie, Ian, Dale, Nora and an elderly thin grey-haired lady who didn't respond. 'I'm a carer,' Douglas said. 'This is my mother. This is my Doris – aren't you darling? (giving her a squeeze) She's got Alzheimer's. Now! – cup of tea? We're having our sitting at 8.30.'

The sitting was in the 'French room' as Douglas called it: a room furnished and decorated in Louis XVI style with an oval walnut table in the centre surrounded by delicate little chairs in velvet and gold leaf. I thought it just as well none of us was fat.

My memory of what actually happened, psychically – if anything – at that first sitting has failed me. Both Vic and I were so touched by the obvious warmth and sincerity of the welcome we received, we found it hard to take in much else. We arranged to go to Douglas's once a week, on a Thursday evening, to sit with the circle, and left with the certainty we'd made a new friend.

Betty Palko was Princess Diana's 'guru' – as the papers called her. For five years from about 1987, Diana, said to be fighting with mental instability

before her separation from Prince Charles, went to Irish-born Mrs. Palko, a clairvoyant medium, for private sittings as often, it was claimed, as once a fortnight. When I saw she was giving a demonstration of clairvoyance at Fulham Spiritualist Church, West London, I decided to go along

Douglas Druce.

and see her and then try to get a topical interview for the paper. I was delayed, and missed her demonstration, but arrived at the church in time to catch her having tea afterwards. She is a small, plump, grey-haired lady with spectacles and a mild manner. She readily agreed for me to interview her. Before I could ask anything about her involvement with Diana she asked me if my father was in spirit and told me he was very close, bringing me a lot of love, and that my mother was there too who 'was a very beautiful lady when she was younger.' She also told me I was 'always typing or doing something.' Perfectly true, I am. But despite being intrigued by what she was saying about me, I'd gone to talk about Princess Diana.

'Princess Diana came to me through recommendation,' Mrs. Palko said. 'I don't advertise my work. I know she will be happy. 1994 will be a wonderful year for her. I think she and Charles will be back together.' As events proved, she was tragically wrong. 'Charles is a very spiritual person,' she continued. 'He used to 'see' a lot when he was a young boy and nobody took much notice of him. I am very much linked with Lord Mountbatten. Princess Diana has a nun for a guide. And so do you – a French nun, very beautiful. She's very very close and brings you a lot of love. You've also got a Chinese philosopher. Are you writing a book?'

She had managed to put the spotlight on me again; whether consciously or not, I don't know. I was quite flattered. And it's true my mother and father are dead; my mother was beautiful; I do a lot of typing; I wasn't writing a book then but it was always in the air. I brought things round to Diana again.

She said: 'I meditate and pray for Charles and Diana every day. I haven't seen her for a while but I think she will come back to me. I used to contact her father, Earl Spencer for her. He gave her advice. I am still in contact with him. Do you suffer with headaches sometimes?'

'Yes, I do.' I could see she didn't want to talk about Princess Diana any more so settled back and happily listened to her talking about me. Quite a lot of what she said was what would commonly be called 'fortune telling': I will go to America, to Egypt. I wouldn't end my days alone: I was going to do an awful lot of research and achieve a lot spiritually and materially, and I could become a medium if I wanted to. Predictions are fairly safe ground. One can't comment on them until they are either proved right or wrong, and for the latter, all things being equal, it's necessary to wait to the last gasp to be absolutely sure. I met Betty Palko again, two years later. At that time none of her predictions for me had come true, except perhaps to a certain extent, the

last one. Now, one, the book, at least, has happened. But – there's still time!
I should certainly like to go to Egypt and America.

We really looked forward to the circle every Thursday evening at Douglas'.
It was a 'physical' circle as distinct from a 'development' circle – like the one
I had been attending in Edmonton. A physical circle is one where attempts
are made to get appraisable effects from discarnate forces: for instance table
tapping, levitation, apports (items which are materialised from the spirit
world) and suchlike. Generally, we learned, a medium should be present to
enhance the possibility of such communication. Douglas's circle had no
medium, although the other sitters and Douglas himself seemed to think Ian,
a tall, rather downbeat young man who ran a cattery, was the medium. Ian
himself obviously thought so too although he was far too modest to say so
outright.

The routine was, we'd all gather in the kitchen, have tea and chat. At 8.30
we'd leave Doris in her chair determinedly gathering the hem of her skirt into
little pleats and then smoothing them out again (repeating the procedure
endlessly) and go into the French room. There we'd sit round the oval table
and blow out the candles. The room was in complete darkness and at first it
was oppressive, although after a few sittings we got used to it. Douglas would
open the circle by asking for communication from our friends in the spirit
world. Then we'd say the Lord's Prayer. Usually nothing would happen for a
while apart from Douglas giving out what he got clairvoyantly – he was
uncannily correct in what he said on many occasions. Then there would be
a rap on the table. That would mean a spirit, or more than one, was present
and wished to speak. Then communication would take place by means of
raps linked to the alphabet – one rap for 'A', two for 'B' and so on. I made
notes after every sitting and these are the notes from our second sitting on 6th
January 1994:

'We began late and there was nothing for a while, then there was a single
knock and when Douglas asked if anyone was there, there was a double
knock and afterwards a scraping noise, loud, from under the table at the foot
of it. Then creaking noises, raps all over the place, some soft, some sharp.
'Zac' was spelled out. Douglas made a joke about Nora (one of the sitters)
going off with one of his pieces of statuary which she'd got her eye on, under
her cloak (because Ian had said he was hearing knocks from behind his chair
in the corner the statue was in), when suddenly the table sort of floated very
quickly in a semi-circular movement away from Ian's direction towards

Douglas and then back again, with scraping noises and taps at the same time. It finished up about a foot further away from me than it began. There were more knocks – eight at one time – and then two sharp knocks which sounded like they were on top of the table, and then more knocks from in front of Victor and me. They didn't make sense, but were very distinct. There was a whistling sound at one stage. We asked if they wanted to close the seance. There were eight knocks, then five. We asked 'Yes?' or 'No?' and they rapped one for 'Yes', so we closed the circle.'

I added a footnote: 'If true – a miracle.'

In all honesty, much as Vic and I enjoyed the evenings at Douglas's, as the séances progressed, week by week, with similar 'phenomena' – taps, table tilting or moving around – we couldn't say we believed it. We were not convinced that one of the sitters wasn't doing it all. Our suspicions fell on Ian. More so when he refused to go in the cabinet – a hardboarded and curtained off corner of the room where ectoplasm is supposed to build up as it emanates from a medium's orifices. Ectoplasm is said to be a white, gauzy substance with a musty odour. Mediums of the past, such as Marjorie Crandon and Helen Duncan (the last person prosecuted in the 1950s under the Witchcraft Act for alleged fraud at a seance), were apparently able to produce this mysterious substance in great quantities, allowing them to build up spirit forms of dead people. As Ian was generally accepted by the circle as being the medium, then Ian should go in the cabinet. But he wouldn't. He said he would feel claustrophobic and be ill – more ill than he was already, which was very ill indeed. On the other hand, we couldn't understand why anyone would want to be bothered to fake all this tapping and pushing tables around every week. There was no money involved, not even any prestige – you couldn't own up to doing it. The question of whether anything that happened at the séances was true, or if Ian was doing it all, or at best helping it along (supposing some part of what was happening was really supernatural) agitated my mind for months. I could come to no conclusion.

One evening we were all sitting round the table in the dark very seriously discussing luminous patches and ectoplasm to be seen in various parts of the room. The table was jiggling about and raps were coming thick and fast, when someone mentioned a 'musty burning smell'. We all smelt it. 'Yes, it's definitely very strong. Must be ectoplasm. That's what it smells like – musty, slightly burnt.' The odour got stronger and stronger. It smelt a bit like school dinners. Everyone became very excited. This was it! Whoever our medium was they were really doing their stuff, exuding tons of ectoplasm. 'It's cabbage,' someone suddenly exclaimed. 'It's old Tom downstairs cooking cabbage!' One of us opened the door of the room a crack. The odour flooded in. Sadly, it most definitely was old Tom in the flat below, over-cooking the cabbage. It smelt awful.

Early in the New Year Vic saw a ghost. He was in bed. He found himself awake at about 4.30 in the morning, but in a trance-like half-awake, half-asleep state; he turned towards the window and saw a woman standing against the closed curtains, half way up them, her feet not on the ground. He saw her quite clearly – a handsome, slim, middle-aged, dark-haired figure with a long nose wearing a blue dress and jacket with padded shoulders and white trimmings and a large brimmed hat, worn slightly to the side, with a small crown bound by a ribbon. His description of the outfit seemed to date it to the late 1930s or early 40s. He said the woman resembled me. As he looked at her, she faded slowly. We wondered if it was my mother.

Doubt, unfortunately, is stronger than belief – at least in my experience. Despite the evidence given by mediums – Mr. Lister, Ida Stenning, Rita Rogers, Keith Surtees; despite Vic's paranormal experience on Paul's birthday in 1992 and his recent sighting of a ghost in the house – it was difficult, almost impossible to believe, or perhaps I should say, maintain belief. Both of us felt this inability to keep faith. Not necessarily with the events at the weekly circle, there were too many grey areas there, but with our own psychic experiences. Yet there was a dichotomy because on looking back at notes and listening again to recordings of the evidence we had received, we could find no rational explanation either.

Then something happened which changed everything. One evening, March 17th 1994, I took my micro-cassette tape recorder along to the circle at Douglas's. It was simply to record the raps and what was said in order to try and determine the veracity of the 'phenomena'. Perhaps the recorder could give me some directional information, or I could detect something through synchronicity – that was the idea. I placed the recorder on the table at the beginning of the session. It had a new tape in it. I switched it on. There were only four of us there that evening – Douglas, Ian, Victor and myself. Three men, one woman. The sitting progressed as usual, some raps, some movement of the table; we chatted ourselves as we usually did. Some days later I played the tape back. About halfway through the tape, in between Douglas saying something and my reply, I heard a woman's voice say my name: 'Judith.' The voice was soft yet sibilant, and there was no doubting it. It was in a tiny gap between us both speaking. I was the only woman present that evening. I didn't say my own name. So who did?

The electronic voice phenomenon, or the EVP as it is usually abbreviated, was discovered – or at least put on the map, I read – by a man named Friedrich Jurgenson. It was 1959. Jurgenson, a Latvian-born documentary film producer, living at that time in Mölnbo, Sweden, had taken his portable tape recorder into woods on his estate to record a finch singing which was needed for the sound track of one of his films. Later when he played the tape he was annoyed to hear a man's voice overlaying the birdsong, speaking in Norwegian and discussing the nocturnal habits of the birds. No-one else had been present in the woods when he made the recording, so he assumed that somehow his tape recorder had acted like a radio receiver picking up somewhere within its circuits a normal radio transmission. Jurgenson continued to make recordings and further strange voices were captured. Some of these addressed him by name and others gave the names of deceased relatives and friends. But the most decisive evidence on tape came when he recorded a female voice speaking to him in German. She said, 'Friedel, my little Friedel, can you hear me?' This was his 'pet' name and he immediately recognised the voice of his mother who had died some four years previously. He was astonished, but now convinced he had established a link with the beyond he continued to make recordings. In 1964 he published a book entitled *Voices from the Universe* in which he describes his views on this phenomenon.

Somehow I too had tapped into this mysterious link with the beyond.

Vic's and Douglas' birthdays fall within a week of each other in April. The house, although by no means finished, was looking far more presentable so we decided to have a joint birthday party. From my point of view it was also a defiant gesture to the beast who stalked in those awful first months after Paul's death. He hadn't been able to devour me – not so far. We thought we'd send out invitation cards and stick on them a photograph of a wine bottle and a glass full of wine surrounded by a haze representing cigarette smoke. It was a gentle hint to bring a bottle. Vic was taking, developing and printing the black and white pictures himself. We set the bottle and glass up on a small table in the first floor front room – the one where I'd fallen into the gap in the floorboards and caused the accident with the ceiling rose. This room was now looking very different – furnished and decorated with beige and cream striped paper. It looked good. Vic spread some sort of gelatine on the photographic plate This would create a hazy, smoky effect when the pictures were printed. He took a number of photographs from different angles and printed them fairly small. We stuck them on the cards, we had about sixty to do.

We'd only done a few when he suddenly said: 'Look at this!' He pointed to one picture, like the others, of the bottle and the glass in front of a background wreathed in 'smoke'. Standing in the curling smoke was a man. His image emerged from the wine glass, faint but distinct, from the waist up. He was about forty-five years old, thin and wiry looking; dishevelled hair falling forward on his lined forehead. He had a rueful look on his face, almost apologetic. He was wearing a crumpled coat with the collar up and possibly a scarf and looked as though he'd been sleeping rough after a heavy night's drinking. We both stared at the picture in amazement. It was the last thing we expected – a spirit on one of our photos. Who was he? When we thought further about this man's image on the photograph, we realised he hadn't appeared on all the others printed from the same exposure. He was only on that one. I got the distinct impression he was from the 1940s era. Other than that we could get no clues. But he was unmistakably there on one of our photographs and he had been captured on camera in the same room where the blankets were mysteriously folded over ornaments on a table just after Christmas 1992. Perhaps he'd been a tenant in the house during the last War. It was highly intriguing. This was one photograph which didn't finish up attached to an invitation card.

An interesting postscript to this is that two years later on one of Douglas' visits, he did automatic writing while I was recording. He began by saying 'Oh, I'm so cold — I'm so cold.' We carried on, he writing, I recording for about ten minutes. On playback, immediately after his second 'I'm so cold' a man's loud gruff voice with a pre-war London accent (which was different from what it is now) had inserted itself saying: 'Well, you would be, I'm in your aura, ain't I?' Was this our spirit in the photo?

After recording the unknown lady saying my name during the circle in March by what I believed was the little known paranormal electronic voice phenomenon, Vic and I decided to sit together twice a week to see if we could record more 'extra' or 'other dimension' voices. We chose the small garden room to use at the far end of the back extension. It still needed a proper slate roof, but it had a temporary felt and pitch one, it was dry and more importantly, quiet. I had done some more reading about the EVP and discovered there were researchers all over the world; the most in Germany with several thousands in two or three societies. In England there appeared to be only a few people interested in the phenomenon. Two of the most prominent were George Bonner in Hastings, Sussex and Raymond Cass in Humberside. They claimed to have recorded thousands of these voices, many addressing them by name, indicating they could see them and knew what they were doing. There was no EVP society in the UK so I wrote to these two gentlemen. There appeared to be two methods for obtaining the voices. One was by using a radio with the dial turned to an unused position on the medium wave between transmissions where only a hissing sound or white noise can be heard. This provided a 'carrier wave' for the voice entities to modulate. The other method was what was called the 'microphone' method, which was simply to use a tape recorder preferably with a remote microphone (in order to avoid picking up the motor noise of the recorder). Somehow or the other the 'voices' would then imprint themselves onto the magnetic tape in the recorder. Jurgenson had picked up his 'voices' using only a tape recorder, therefore by employing the microphone method, without a radio, and so inadvertently, had I. The whole thing was almost beyond belief. Yet, a mysterious woman had spoken to me out of thin air. Her voice there on tape. Anyone could hear it. It wasn't the voice of one of the people who were present at the circle that evening – Douglas, Vic or Ian – and it wasn't me. This phenomenon had to be investigated. I was hooked.

Stephen Holbrook is a young clairaudient medium from Wakefield in Yorkshire. Clairaudience means hearing rather than seeing spirits. Some other people from Yorkshire whom I'd met during the Lynwood Fellowship week in Castleton had mentioned him and said he was marvellous and packing them into the churches up in Wakefield and surrounding districts. They wrote and told me he was coming to Hitchin Spiritualist Church, about twenty miles north of London. It looked as if his fame had spread, as people were streaming into the new but nondescript church in a back street. I took a seat at the side quite near to the front with a good view. I wanted to record the demonstration and write a piece for the paper. I asked the President of the Church to announce I was there, and what I was doing, and to ask people who received 'messages' from Stephen to come and see me afterwards to give me their names and phone numbers so I could ring them the following day to get their impressions and observations as to the accuracy of the information they'd received.

After the President had delivered his address, and an expectant wait of about ten minutes, Stephen bounced onto the platform. He was young, twenty-seven years old, a hairdresser, his blonde hair tied into a pony-tail. Although he was beaming I could see he was nervous, and who could blame him? This youthful crimper was facing a sea of devouring eyes, willing him to come to them with a message from a loved dead one.

He began hesitantly, head to one side, listening, commenting on the private voices he heard: 'Ah, yes — OK. I'll tell her. Right!' as though he was on the telephone: singling out recipients, giving them unusual information – how much money one woman had in her handbag; another was told she'd just dyed her hair and Arthur, in the spirit world, liked it the way it was before. The lady who this message was for clearly couldn't make up her mind what was more important – her hurt vanity or the message proving her dear departed was still around. Another was told what item of clothing she had picked up to wear before leaving home and then discarded. A man was greeted by his friend Bill who had lost half his forefinger in an accident at work and was wanting to be remembered to him. The man this message was given to reacted with amazement. As Stephen worked, he began to relax, to gain confidence. Information flowed through him to the audience. It was not vague and generalised of the 'Take it with you and think about it dear' variety. It was specific, humorous and accurate. Trivia tailored to the recipients, meaning something to them only. The demonstration was impressive. Obviously everyone else thought so too. At the end he received enthusiastic applause. I looked forward to hearing people's personal reactions.

One of the people who came to see me after the demonstration was an elderly lady named René. She had received a message and wanted to tell me how pleased she was with it and how accurate it was. She gave me her telephone number. I said I'd ring her the next day and chat. I phoned as promised, attaching my micro-cassette recorder to the phone via a pick-up coil stuck on the receiver by suction pad to record the two-way conversation. René rambled on quite a bit, but I dutifully recorded it all and later played the tape back prior to transcribing it. I was mentally deleting most of what had been said as irrelevant when, in a tiny gap in the middle of her answer to one of my questions, I heard a hoarse whispered voice say 'Harry!' She had been saying something about her father, so I ran the tape back and listened again carefully. Her actual words were:

'My father died a long time ago. He used to contact me all the time, but all of a sudden the messages from him stopped. And my young brother has been doing this business since he was seventeen…' I interrupt with: 'What business?' René says 'Er…' and the 'extra' voice jumps in with 'Harry!' spoken very close to the microphone. Then René continues: '…spiritualism.'

Intrigued, I phoned her back the next day. I reminded her she had been talking about her father and brother and asked her what their names were. She said: 'Well, my brother is Edward, and my father was Henry John, but everyone called him Harry.' This was interesting. It appeared that EVP could operate on the telephone as well, or it could be (given that I accepted a paranormal voice had stated René's father's name) that the entity or other dimensional voice, call it what you will, had spoken directly into my tape recorder via the inbuilt mike, but had obviously heard the two-way telephone conversation in order for the remark to be relevant. It seemed incredible. I thought again about the time the answering machine had phoned John back in the dark days of 1992. Perhaps it was spirit intervention and not some fault in the mechanism. The idea seemed a little more feasible now.

There was a dry-cleaning shop opposite our house. The shop subsequently turned itself into a second-hand satellite dish outlet run by the same proprietor. There's probably more money in dirty dishes than dirty clothes. When the shop was still a dry-cleaners a local woman helped out in it occasionally. She was usually drunk, chain smoking and very unpleasant indeed. From my vantage point at my window opposite, behind the net curtains, I often saw people in disputes with her. I think the shop owner kept her there to drive customers away so he'd have a good excuse to close down and re-open as something more lucrative. At Douglas' circle one Thursday evening, Douglas 'saw' a large new silvery spanner and a nut. Unusual things to see clairvoyantly, we all thought. The next day, from a different vantage point, this time the first-floor front window which I happened to be cleaning from the inside at the time, I saw to my surprise the unsavoury assistant having a huge row with someone inside the shop. The next moment the man she was screaming at dashed out, cursing her, and she followed him down the street, walking like a wooden puppet on a string – jerkily and weirdly. But the strangest thing of all was that in her hand she held the largest shiniest silver spanner I'd ever seen. 'A nut with a spanner, just as Douglas said,' I thought wryly.

At 10.30 every Sunday and Wednesday evening Vic and I retired to the back room, closed the curtains, arranged the two chairs on opposite sides of a small wooden table, lit a candle in a bottle placed on the table and set down my thirteen-year-old Aiwa micro-cassette recorder, switched to 'record: high volume'. We then blew out the candle and were in pitch darkness. We were sitting for the EVP and trying to create the same conditions that had encouraged the first 'voice' to say my name. Nothing happened for quite a long time. Several weeks went by and all we experienced was the stifling airlessness and heavy blackness of sitting in a small room with anywhere that could let in light and air covered. The room was so quiet we suffered from sensory deprivation unless we talked all the time, so even if any entity had spoken on tape we probably wouldn't have heard them in the midst of our babble. After a few weeks, we calmed down, let some light and air in and left spaces on the tape for 'voices' to speak to us.

One evening in June, after a very hot day, we had our usual session. It was unbearably close in the room and both of us agreed we'd had a strange feeling in our bodies like an electric current running through. We were glad to get out at the end of an hour and get some fresh air. I ran the tape back and began to listen to it. At 201-2 on the counter, to my amazement, I heard a man's voice say quite clearly: 'I've been every week.' I called for Vic. He rushed in. We both listened intently. It was definitely there. I didn't tell Vic what I'd heard, he repeated what the man said: 'I've been every week.' We looked at each other wide-eyed. 'Who is it?' we said simultaneously.

After that someone spoke to us at almost every sitting. We even recognised certain voices. Vic had a rather pompous young man who would make remarks like 'Upsetting!' or 'Keep it up' on the occasions when, in the course of our discussions on tape, he would get worked up about politics or social attitudes. I often had a woman comment on things I had said. It may have been the same woman who initially spoke my name. She had a gentle voice with a slight west country accent. During one session one of the cats miaowed to be let in through the french windows. I opened them and let him in, saying as I did: 'What are you doing?' The apt comment on tape by my gentle-voiced woman was 'Looking in the dark!'

At first, we were so excited by these discarnate participants at our sittings we ran the tapes backwards and forwards to listen and listen again to their few words. This resulted in the words being distorted and often eventually rubbed out completely. This nearly happened to one of the most remarkable sentences we recorded. We had our sitting in the usual way, with the bottle on the table and a candle in it. We were in the dark, and I inadvertently caught the bottle with my elbow making it wobble with a 'djoing-djoing' noise before it righted itself. When we listened to the tape of that evening's sitting, we heard a man's voice with a very broad Irish accent say: 'That was a narrow escape, you nearly broke the bottle!' It was a brilliantly clear sentence and the longest we had recorded so far. We played it over and over again, enthralled by the knowledge that whoever the owner of this voice might be, he wasn't in our dimension and was certainly in another – wherever that was. At our next sitting we asked who he was, where he was, but he didn't speak again.

About this time, I thought it would be a good idea to find some paid employment. I'd done voice-over recordings before and I had a good demo tape so I decided I'd try and find some work. Cash flow was getting to be a problem and the cats had expensive tastes. I sent copies of my tape in various directions and had the usual junk mail delivered every day, but no enthusiastic would-be employers, except one. Talking Books for the Blind. I phoned them up. They said they'd love me to read for their *Talking Newspaper*. 'Where is the studio located?' I asked. 'Haringey,' they said. 'That's north of me, quite close,' I thought. However, there was just one problem. They didn't pay. But I couldn't weasel out of it, so one week later in the studio (actually located in the Council Offices), I'm reading for the local Phoenix Group's *Talking Newspaper*!

There were a number of other people reading as well. We took it in turns to read articles out of the local paper. Each session was recorded onto cassettes and delivered to interested blind and disabled people by Council services. One of the other volunteers was a man named Dennis Gunn. He was tall with black hair and a beard. He looked like a Naval officer. I knew immediately Douglas and he would like each other and made up my mind to introduce them. But whilst talking to Dennis I discovered he'd had a number of intriguing psychic experiences which I thought would make a good piece for the paper. I arranged to go to his house one afternoon and make a recording of him relating one or two of them. He is an astral traveller and this is one of his journeys:

'One night I awoke out of my body thinking it was me, the physical me, waking up. In fact it's the astral body waking up. A feeling of lightness and freedom. A wonderful feeling. I remember going to this place. I didn't particularly want to go. My feet were on a canal bank with a bridge over it. People were paddling in the canal up to their knees. It was a pretty dull, boring, dismal place – ordinary. Dark red bricks like a Lowry painting – mundane. Suddenly a man appeared at the side of me. He just said to me: "What are you doing here?" I didn't query who he was. He just appeared. I said, "I'm just hanging around," and he said, "Hold on to me." I held on to his left arm with both hands. I could feel his arm. He was a little bit smaller than me – about 5' 8" or 5' 9". He whisked me away to another plane. I felt he was a guide who'd come down to take me to a higher plane to show me there are other levels of existence that one can go to. I think the message to me was, "You can only achieve this higher state if you spiritually progress whilst here on earth. If you help other people and think less of yourself and more of others, this will be a good thing for your spirit when you pass over." On the left of us was a row of iron railings amongst this dismal landscape. We zoomed towards these railings at high speed and went straight through them. And then he and I were there, at the most glorious place. Glorious technicolour. A river of mercury. It was so thick, so silver. Grass banks greener than green. Emerald. Emerald green leaves on trees. Men, women and children smiling, happy, frolicking; little dogs rolling on the embankment. The sky was silver and blue. Like a painting. Like MGM, every musical you'd ever seen. Hollywood. The colours were vibrant. And you stood there and watched. He looked at me looking. I was amazed and I looked at him – youngish fellow. He was a messenger. He wanted me to see such places existed so I could say to other people, disbelievers, that when you pass on one door closes another opens. I knew it was the spirit world. I looked at him and I said "I'm dead, I'm dead," and with saying so I said to myself "Oh, fantastic! Why didn't I die years ago?" The feeling of freedom and happiness was so lovely. I didn't want to go back to that earth or that body in that bed. I wanted to be there. It was a feeling of absolute – it's not an earthly feeling. He looked at me and said, "Not dead. In the land of." I bathed in the glory of it all. Religion didn't come into it. I got the message that this was the place I could go to if I chose. I said to myself, "I must go back and tell my friend" – I was sharing the house with him – and I then left the dimension and came back into my room. I came in backwards. You see your body in bed. You know the two have to merge – eyelash for eyelash, fingernail for fingernail. I wondered how I'd get through the sheets. But I did. I wasn't afraid. I came in with a sigh. It was very relaxing. I felt wonderful.'

Dennis speaks so concisely that all I had to do was type out his story straight from the recorder. It hardly needed editing. I got to the place on tape where he says: 'He whisked me away to another plane...' and at that point I heard another male voice, far lighter and younger than Dennis's, say: 'I want you to know'. So someone else had been listening to the story and added his comment. This time I wasn't quite so amazed to hear the voice, I was beginning to get used to the idea that 'they' were always around. I welcomed it. I was waiting for the day to arrive when Paul would speak. Surely he must!

August that year was surprisingly hot, too hot to stay cooped up in London breathing trapped exhaust fumes. Vic had taken a couple of weeks off and was in the Midlands with his band playing some gigs. A friend, who'd been abroad and I hadn't seen for a while, rang up and asked if I'd like to go out of town on a long hike. I agreed enthusiastically. I really enjoy walking, especially using Ordnance Survey maps and seeing all those footpaths, stiles, and areas of special interest come to life. As Martin and I got off the train at Southminster in Essex, the sun blazed down. There was nobody around. The station appeared to be behind the village, some distance away, in a sort of no-man's land. The train rattled off and we sniffed fresh air appreciatively and surveyed the scene. Dengie marshes were our target; echoes of Dickens' *Great Expectations* when the boy Pip finds the convict who's his unknown benefactor, looming up on him out of the mist. Dickens set his book in Romney Marshes in another part of the country, in Kent, and there wasn't any mist today, but this kind of flat, desolate landscape has a mournful fascination in the best of weather. We spread out the map and chose our route – Tillingham Marsh and the coast. Hitching up our rucksacks we set off.

It was such a lovely, golden day. Corn waved in fields, weathered old bricks on deserted Howe Farm glowed warmly. We passed an empty cottage standing alone in the flat landscape, its front door open, paint peeling off. Who could have lived there? we wondered. Was the building old enough to have housed one of those farmers from the last century who had to keep finding new wives as their brides sickened and died from marsh fever? At one time too the area had seen a lot of violence arising from smuggling on the marshes. If only bricks could speak. We walked on, checking with the map that Tillingham Marsh was on our left; ahead of it, nearer to the sea, were a series of duck decoy ponds. I wondered if they were still in use. What a shame for the ducks.

'What's that?' Martin said suddenly, pointing ahead and to the right. I shaded my eyes and peered into the far distance. It looked like two figures, dressed in black, at the edge of a path. They seemed to be idly circling each other on bikes, but they were so far away we could only see them as black dots. An alarm bell rang in my mind. *Yobs, looking for trouble. That's the last thing I need. Why are they everywhere? The one consolation is Martin will soon see them off, he's a big bloke. But what if they've got a gun? You never know these days.* I glanced at Martin. He wasn't worried. We carried on walking towards the figures. The strange thing was that as we got closer and closer they didn't change in size, and seemed to merge into one. We walked for about ten minutes, all the time approaching the black figure but not nearing it. It was the oddest sensation, as though you were walking yet standing still. The figure remained motionless, the same size and completely black. No detail of form or clothing emerged. Suddenly it moved very quickly in a sort of gliding, loping movement up the rising cornfield which lay behind it. The arms were outstretched as though on a horse or motorbike, yet there was no sound whatsoever. In a second it crossed the field in great bounds and arrived at the top on a ridge where it appeared to turn and watch us. As we cleared a mound to our right which hid it, and climbed onto the marsh defence sea wall running alongside the duck decoy ponds, we looked back. The figure was still there, still the same size, black and motionless.

There were some war-time pillboxes near the sea wall. I wondered whether what we had seen could have been a ghost – something to do with the war and the RAF. Perhaps a motorcycle courier, though what he would have been doing out on Dengie marshes I don't know. But Martin and I both agreed the figure hadn't behaved like it was flesh and blood. If it had been a misty eerie day we could have perhaps accounted for it as a figment of an over-active imagination heightened by climatic conditions. But it was a lovely, bright day with perfect long distance visibility. The verdict was – very peculiar!

When Vic returned I told him about the encounter on the marshes and at the next sitting we asked about the figure. Vic says on tape (referring to it) 'We must find out about that.' Later he says, 'Incredible actually. Those things are amazing.' On playback, 'voices' had imprinted on the tape at these two points. At the first point – 'we must find out about that' – a male voice immediately says: 'Keep away from me!' and at the second, the same voice whispers in a slow, drawn-out way behind the words 'incredible actually' one word – 'h-a-u-n-t-i-n-g'. This recording didn't prove the existence or otherwise of a ghost on Dengie marshes. I would very much like to know whether anyone else has ever seen such a figure there. But it did prove one thing again – we were definitely recording voices from somewhere in the universe by the EVP.

At the end of August, on the 26th, the night before the second anniversary of Paul's death, I had the first of a series of vivid dreams. This one was taking place in the Savoy hotel in London. I was in the sitting room of a two-bedroom suite waiting for someone else to arrive. I wasn't sure who, except that it was a man. I went into each of the bedrooms and saw a dead man in each of the two beds. I hid both the corpses under the floorboards and when the man I was waiting for came back I didn't tell him straight away. When I did tell him police were called and I was questioned and realised I'd be charged with murder. I found the whole thing very amusing and remember thinking that now I'd be famous and my name would be headlines.

When I woke up I remembered the dream and had a horrible thought that perhaps it was symbolic, representing my two sons, and that something was going to happen to Vic that would be my fault. Later I bought the *Evening Standard* and there was an article in it headed 'The Fight for the Savoy'. It was about two men – one of them Charles Forté – who wanted to take control of the hotel. As far as I know neither one of them finished up murdered and underneath the floorboards!

The next dream was on the night of Paul's birthday, September 13th. I found myself on a high floor of a large building or boat and on looking out of the window saw the sea covered in green growth, like algae or seaweed – dark big clumps of it heaving under the surface, coming right up to the wall of the structure we were in. And the depth of the sea was unfathomable. It was sinister. The next scene in the dream shifted to me trying to find a toilet, but every toilet room I went into had a bed in it and the rooms were ramshackle. Garish colours, yellow doors, bits of blue wood tacked together. The last room I entered had a dirty bed occupying most of it with the toilet against the right hand wall but impossible to get to because the bed was in the way. And the bed had a thin mauve nylon counterpane on it and underneath, obviously, was a person moving around although the whole body was covered, even the face. I glanced up at the ceiling, and it was bulging as though water had collected above it and was about to burst through. Next, I was sitting near a young man and I said 'Where is this place?' He said, 'Island, of course: nine ghosts'.

When I woke up and thought about this dream, which was still vividly in my mind, I couldn't make anything of it at all. Two weeks later on the twenty-eighth of the same month a roll-on roll-off ferry *The Estonia* went down in the Baltic Sea at 1.30 am. Nine hundred people were believed drowned in very deep waters near a small island. It was apparently a very high boat and most of the people were asleep and trapped in their cabins when it sank. I don't know if my dream bore any relation to this dreadful accident soon to happen, or if it was just coincidence.

Three months later I had another dream foretelling another accident, this time a plane crash. Perhaps one looks for signs and portents when in a heightened state of awareness which I was obviously in, or perhaps the signs and portents are always there but not observed because one's normal state is possibly closer to torpor than anything else – perhaps due to all the pollutants in the atmosphere.

Just before Paul died in the late summer of 1992 Vic and I went to Portugal for a week. His fiancée had gone home to Germany and we were both at a loose end. It was a strange, gloomy week despite the sun. A shadow seemed to be hanging over us. I remember wanting to phone Paul for no particular reason, then telling myself I was being stupid. He'd be all right. Why shouldn't he be? Vic was sensing problems ahead with his girlfriend. One afternoon just before we came home, Vic jumped up and drew a large eye in the sand with a stick, and the words 'I See' written underneath. I asked what it meant, why he'd drawn it. He said there was no reason, he just felt like doing it. I took a photograph of the drawing.

At the end of October two years later when so much had changed for ever, I was glancing at a leaflet from The World Goodwill Forum outlining their forthcoming events. I noticed, under 'Festival Meditation Meetings London 1994' two sub-headings. One read: 'Taurus – 25th April' (this is Vic's astrological sign). The quotation next to it read: 'I see and when the eye is open all is light'. The other heading was entitled: 'Cancer – 22nd July' (my sign) and it read: 'I build a lighted house and therein I dwell'. Recalling the eye in the sand and the last two years of grindingly hard work in the house, these two maxims struck me as totally apposite.

Eel Pie Island is a minuscule little blob of land in the River Thames where it snakes round West London at Twickenham. I had a friend living there whom I hadn't seen for years. Her name was René Stephens. She had two children named Sybil and Peter who weren't children any more. Sybil was married and Peter had become a meteorologist living in Papua New Guinea. René doted on Peter. He was the youngest, the only son and now thousands of miles away. On impulse, I set off to visit her. She knew Paul and Vic but hadn't seen either of them since they were small. She would want to know Paul had died. I knocked on the door of Kent Lodge on the island and it was opened by a huge dog dragging a woman on a lead. The woman regarded me suspiciously (the dog would have liked to kill me). I asked for René. The woman told me René had left and she was the new owner of the house. I asked if would she mind giving me René's new address. It was in Spain. I exclaimed with surprise that I didn't think she would ever leave Eel Pie Island, but to go as far away as Spain – that didn't sound like her. The woman replied: 'No, she probably wouldn't, but her son died five years ago in a car accident and she wanted to move far away.'

Peter dead! How tragic! I walked slowly away from the island, across the wooden bridge. *René must be devastated. He had died in a car accident. Poor Peter. Five years ago. Five years! I thought, that means he died before Paul! Who was it the medium Rita Rogers said 'took Paul over'? It was Peter! I didn't know any Peter who had died at that time. Now I do.* I found myself beside the river. Glancing over to the other bank I noticed a Thames barge moored there. It's name painted on the side in blue letters was *Peter Peter.*

The late Samuel C. R. Alsop wrote a book about EVP entitled *Whispers of Immortality.* It's a good read, although if I hadn't had personal experience of the phenomenon, I think it would have been hard to swallow. He claimed two-way conversations with departed friends and even pictures of the dead on television. But, having learnt there's 'more twixt heaven and hell than meets the eye', I found what he had to say struck some chords. He mentioned he believed in the existence of a spirit transmitting station named Rada Peter to which one could tune by using an interfrequency position on a radio dial and obtaining the white noise or hissing sound and then simply asking someone at the spirit station to speak. A couple of days prior to this I'd seen a programme on television about how the twenty-first century will develop. The professor in the programme quoted special numbers which come up mathematically randomly in the chaos theory of the universe. I made a note of these numbers; there were four of them. It seemed a good idea to ask Rada Peter if they could give me another two to make up six needed for the lottery which I hadn't the faintest hope of winning, never having won anything in my life. So I found an appropriate position on the radio, knelt down by it and with my face about half an inch away asked my spirit friends in Rada Peter to give me two more numbers for the lottery. I nearly fainted when a voice spoke from the radio giving numbers. It was a man's voice and I thought he said 'One, three, three, one,' then a pause, then 'nine.' Vic, who'd been sitting on the sofa but leapt to his feet when heard the faint crackling voice, thought he said 'One, three, four, eight,' then a pause, then 'nine'. The whole episode only lasted a millisecond and afterwards we wondered if we'd imagined it. But I made combinations of the numbers we thought we'd heard and added them to the four numbers I had from the programme. The following Saturday I won £10 on the lottery.

Up to now we'd been using just my Aiwa micro-cassette tape recorder at our EVP sittings. One evening, in early November, we recorded what sounded like Paul's voice saying, 'It's green,' and then later in the tape 'It's metering.' We got very excited by these two cryptic messages, but the information itself was meaningless. What is 'green' and what is 'metering'? – unless the last word was a reference to the tape recorder counter. But why should Paul's first words to us be so banal? For that matter, why should any of the entities whose voices had miraculously appeared from another dimension onto magnetic tape in a tape recorder by some process unknown and undreamed of, talk such trivia, as for the most part, they had. They should first of all give us their name (which hardly ever happens), then tell us what it's like to go towards the light we've all heard about, if they saw Jesus, whether they met grandma and grandad, if the family dog or cat is there? and a million other things of immense importance to us poor souls still waiting to shuffle off this mortal coil and full of fear. Still, we didn't think Paul, when he finally spoke to us – and he *must* speak to us – would waste precious time and energy on banalities. So we reluctantly dismissed this first contact: it was not from him.

Then I dropped the tape recorder on an uncarpeted floor. It didn't break into pieces. It looked all right. But for our next sitting, we borrowed someone's expensive recording equipment and remote microphone. The microphone was so remote it allowed us to hang it up in the back room and put the equipment itself fifty feet away in the sitting room. This machine used a normal size cassette, so we put in a new 60-minute TDK tape and began to record. We crept into the back room, seated ourselves at the small table and began the session. It was a bit daunting, like being in a BBC studio knowing every small sound would be picked up by the impressive looking microphone hanging above our heads, and you couldn't afford to make any mistakes. Vic began to tell me about an incident which had happened when he had been mixing up some cellulose filler earlier in the day in the kitchen.

He said: 'I'd just mixed up the Polyfilla and I was thinking about Paul, when there was a loud bang from inside the kitchen cupboard.'

I replied, in a facetious way: 'Oh, it wasn't Paul making the bang from the kitchen cupboard, the Polyfilla you'd mixed up went hard and you dropped it and that was what made the loud noise.'

Vic, who wasn't in the mood for flippant remarks, said rather sourly: 'Yes, well, can you not…' and trailed off the retort, as one does – left it hanging in mid-air, its meaning clear.

We carried on chatting and leaving the usual gaps for a further twenty minutes or so, then closed the session, returned to the sitting room and switched off the recorder. We sat down to listen to the playback. It was crystal clear. We could hear our footsteps returning down the long corridor from the sitting room after switching the tape on. We heard the door of the back room open and close; the shuffling sound as we sat down; even my stomach rumbling. We heard ourselves say the Lord's Prayer which we usually begin with – my voice always a little behind Vic's as he gallops through it. Then he began his story about the Polyfilla. I laughed a little as he told it and chuckled when I said: 'The 'Polyfilla' you'd mixed up went hard and you dropped it and that was what made the loud noise.' We then heard Vic say: 'Yes, well, can you not...' But, amazingly, the sentence didn't finish there. It was completed and it now said: 'Yes, well, can you not *laugh at us,*' and the words 'laugh at us' were in Paul's voice.

It was unmistakably and without any shadow of doubt his voice. Although they were brothers and had a similar tone, the intonation, accent and speed were completely different. Vic went to boarding school in Dorset in the west of England and has a trace of the local accent. Paul went to a London school and adopted the vernacular. Vic speaks fairly slowly. Paul spoke very quickly. Even the sentiment expressed in the rounded-off sentence was Paul's. 'Don't laugh at us,' he was saying 'at my brother and me.' Fiercely partisan: protective of his younger brother. We could even hear the slight whistle behind the words which was caused by his front tooth (the one Vic had shown to the medium, Mr. Lister) being out.

Both of us were completely overwhelmed. We'd heard from Paul. He'd spoken to us two years after his death. *He's not dead!* We ran the tape back again and again to reassure ourselves it was him. It was absolutely amazing. Remembering how we'd almost destroyed other voices on the smaller cassettes, we immediately copied this one, repeating the sentence over and over to make sure we couldn't lose it. I felt like crying and laughing at the same time. In fact I did. I wanted more: a conversation with him. I wanted to see him, to tell him I loved him; to ask him what he's doing, where he is. We sat by the expensive recording equipment as though it was the dearest friend in the world. It had brought us Paul. We loved it.

Getting technical

Just before 1994 ended, I had a third vivid dream. It was on the night of the 18th of December. In my dream it was daylight and I was standing on the pavement outside a row of modern houses on the edge of what appeared to be a housing estate. There was a wooded copse opposite. Above the tree line, about a mile away, I saw a small plane explode in mid-air. I heard the word 'Heathrow' and knew the plane would crash at an airport. On December 21st a cargo plane crashed in a wood just outside Coventry Airport. Five people were killed. The crash occurred in daylight, a short distance from a housing estate.

Generally my dreams are not like this. They're a jumbled up adaptation of something that has happened, or I've seen or heard, during the day. Why I had these three prophetic dreams about the Savoy, *The Estonia* and now this, I don't know. I think it was Einstein who compared time to being on an endless road. If you could see all of the road at the same time – if you were an eye out in space – you would see everything and everybody that ever existed or ever will exist on it travelling along, each passing a different event landmark, but all at the same time. This means that everything that is going to happen has happened already, which would explain pre-cognitive dreams, but not why random people like myself have them and what they have them for. In my frame of reference, I think the dreams I had were to reinforce my growing and grateful realisation of heightened psychic awareness.

Early in the New Year I met George Bonner. We'd both gone to an inaugural meeting in Oxford of an embryonic EVP society. Along with Ray Cass, he was one of the people to whom I'd written after the first EVP voice saying my name had imprinted on tape. In the event, the society didn't get off the ground, but George (who lived in Hastings, Sussex) and I kept up a correspondence and met a few times, and I learned a great deal about the electronic voice phenomenon from him. George was undoubtedly one of the prime movers of the EVP: a psychotherapist and artist who began full-time research into the phenomenon in 1972 after reading a copy of a book by a Latvian parapsychologist, Dr. Konstantin Raudive. Dr. Raudive had studied Friedrich

Jurgenson's discovery of his ability to record spirit voices, and his methods, and had gone on to make over 100,000 recordings himself of apparent paranormal voices.

Dr. Raudive initially felt the phenomenon could be explained as the researcher's own subconscious deluding his conscious mind. However, after meeting Jurgenson and participating in his experiments, he soon came to believe that the unexplained voices captured on magnetic tape were indeed the voices of the dead. He returned to Germany where he was living, and went on to record many thousands of his own 'extra' voices and publish a book in German in 1971. This was translated by British publisher Colin Smythe under the new title *Breakthrough: An Amazing Experiment in Electronic Communication with the Dead*. Colin Smythe was the person to coin the term Electronic Voice Phenomenon (EVP) soon after publication of the English translation of Raudive's book. He initially called the 'voices' 'Raudive Voices' but decided this description was misleading as Dr. Raudive had not been the discoverer of the phenomenon. 'Aeriel voices', as they were first called, were recorded on tape in the USA in 1956, according to a report sent to the American Association for Psychic Research by Californian artist and psychic researcher Raymond Bayless in 1959, and published in their winter journal. His report concerned the experiments of Hollywood photographer and independent

Colin Smythe (left) and Dr Konstantin Raudive. Photo courtesy of Colin Smythe.

voice medium Atilla von Szalay who claimed to have made the recording. Strangely, the publication of this discovery produced no response or interest whatsoever.

But the story of the EVP probably began even earlier than this, at the beginning of the century, with those eminent scientists Edison, Marconi and Tesla who laid the foundations upon which electronics has been based. All were interested in the possibility of electronic communication with the dead and spent the final years of their lives trying to develop devices to enable this to be a reality. However, it was Dr. Raudive's book which focused the English speaking world on the amazing possibility that the dead could speak to us. At first there was a flurry of interest; interviews, articles, television programmes: then critics came forward intent on rubbishing his findings. His 'voices' were dismissed as mistaken radio signals, radio frequency atmospherics, projections of the mind, wishful thinking, hallucinations or Super ESP.

George Bonner wrote in 1993:

'I must confess that, as one trained in psychology, my first reaction was that either the author of *Breakthrough* was self-deluded or else had set out deliberately to deceive his readers. However, using my reel to reel tape recorder and battery radio I set about making a recording as described by Raudive. "Can anyone hear me?" I asked, speaking into the microphone and "Would anyone like to speak to me?" I heard nothing and felt rather foolish and a little dejected, even though I had expected nothing. I re-wound the tape and replayed it. My voice came over the speaker loud and clear – "Can anyone hear me?" and "Would anyone like to speak to me?" There was a hiss and rush of sound and then a voice shouted to me, sounding as if someone was calling down a long tunnel "YES!" I will always remember this voice, the first of over 50,000 I have since recorded. It is still on my archival tapes. It was this voice that began my own research into the voice phenomenon. I soon came to realise that it was not just the question of suitable electronics, although one did require the correct apparatus and also the knowledge of its use; but most important was patience and determination to succeed; also one's own psychological attitude. Although many of the voices which were recorded could be heard and understood quite clearly, others were whisper type voices and some came buried in a high noise level of radio static and mush. It demanded considerable skill and patience to listen at length to this, in order to spot paranormal voices that could lie hidden between such sounds.

'Obviously the study of EVP would be something that appealed to a more

Gilbert George Bonner. Photo courtesy *Hastings Observer*.

specialised field, to the more intelligent type of person unable to accept the theories of a materialistic science. My aim, however, was to try and establish the audio-reality of the voices and to persuade parapsychologists to investigate this research which I felt had much to teach us. Whether these were voices of the dead, some manifestation of the unconscious mind, or even the voices of some "extraterrestrials" seemed to me to be of secondary importance. The first priority was to establish the voices' existence on tape and not merely something dreamed up by imagination. I suppose to some extent I succeeded in that such a well known parapsychologist as Professor H. Bender, then of the University of Freiburg, Germany heard some of my voices and commented on their clarity. Other research and tapes went to the Electronic Warfare Division of a major US Air Base. These were later sent to Dr. William Braud of The Mind Science Foundation in Texas, USA.

'In 1981 Dr. Braud gave a lecture in Dallas and published a paper on "The Electronic Voice Phenomenon" in which he gave a positive approach to this work, mentioning in his report my own contribution.

'Here in the UK unfortunately parapsychologists as a group have shown an amazing reluctance to have anything at all to do with the EVP. No doubt they are aware it poses awkward questions for them – questions for which they have no answers, certainly within the framework of their own field of study.

A couple of years ago I demonstrated to members of the Society for Psychical Research how, under test conditions and on a tape supplied by them, I could record EVP voices in their presence. Voices came through giving my name and also that of Raudive. All three people present heard and agreed the interpretation, but in spite of this evidence they dismissed the voices as merely projection. One cannot make progress faced with such illogical and negative attitudes.

'I do realise, of course, that the question as to whether these voices do come from the dead is one that is well open to dispute. I make no claims. I merely state that some of the voices do identify themselves as spirit entities. Since we cannot as yet explain how the voices are recorded, or their origin, I feel it might not be unreasonable to listen to what they say since the whole purpose of communication is the exchange of information. This, I admit, may not be accepted as proof – but evidence of something it certainly is.

'Although most people now accept the existence of ESP and also telepathy, many doubt the possibility of life after death. This is a complex question that depends on the exact nature of the relationship between the mind and the brain – on this opinions differ. The evidence of OOB's (out of body experiences) and that of NDE's (near death experiences) taken together with that of other PSI research, suggests it is a possibility that has to be considered seriously, even though it conflicts with established scientific thinking.

'The evidence of the paranormal takes us beyond science to concepts of reality in which may lie hidden the secrets of life itself.'

By the beginning of the New Year my cherished Aiwa tape recorder which I had so carelessly dropped, conked out completely. Before it finally died, it had managed to record even more EVP voices than before. One communication was very amusing and impressive. It occurred one afternoon when I was alone in the house. The power kept failing and I had to continually go down to the cellar and re-set the trip switch to get it restored again. I was so fed up with this to-ing and fro-ing that after one of my visits to the cellar I decided to try a little experiment and switched on the tape recorder in the kitchen; speaking into the recorder I asked our friends in another dimension, 'Is it one of you on the other side turning off our electricity?' I re-wound and played the tape, and what I heard in answer to my question, uttered by a very emphatic, tetchy, elderly man's voice was: 'Don't recognise who *you* is?' The implication was I should have addressed whoever was tampering with the electricity by name and I had committed some grave social error by not doing so. The remark was so precise and formal, yet in tone and content expressed so much, I could imagine my unseen gentleman, if he had been there in the flesh, to be an old colonel type, with a red face and handlebar moustaches which he would have twirled impatiently because of my impertinence.

Psychic World eventually proved too much for Simon although he had done an excellent job in producing it – on the odd occasions when it appeared. In January 1995 the paper was taken over by a new owner and editor and its first front page was a story of mine about the EVP. A few days after the paper had been published, I received a phone call from a man in Dundee, Scotland named Norval Fyall. He said he was 62 years old and a retired caretaker. He had read my article and wanted to tell me of his amazing experience with the phenomenon. He sounded very excited. He said he was coming to London and could he see me? I gladly agreed and on February 14th he came to my house and told me the following story:

'My wife Valerie died at the age of 59 in May last year. I thought I'd go before her as I've got advanced cancer, but it wasn't to be. Before she died she promised to try and communicate with me from the other side. I didn't think I'd be able to live without her so I asked her, if I couldn't cope, whether it would be all right if I came over – meaning I might commit suicide. Neither of us had any interest in or knowledge of spiritualism, nor were we particularly religious.

'When Valerie died, I was in despair. My son David suggested a holiday in Malta and we were booking up at the travel agents when I suddenly changed my mind and said I'd visit some German friends of mine in Bavaria instead. During the visit, seeing how depressed I was, the wife of the German couple suddenly asked me if I'd like to talk to Valerie. She told me she'd read of a man in another part of Germany who was continually in touch with his dead father by means of the EVP. Should she ring him for me? My mind boggled. What on earth was the EVP anyway? I was a complete sceptic, but so miserable I would have tried anything. I agreed. The advice she got from the man (whose name was Manfred) was to buy a Philips variable speed tape recorder (which I couldn't find in Scotland and had to order from Germany), and tune my radio to what is called 'white noise' – the radio mush obtained at a point half-way between stations. I then had to record a short message on the tape and wait for results.

'On my return to Dundee, feeling full of doubt and an absolute fool, I did as instructed, using a small cassette recorder I already had. I recorded a short message of love to my wife, tuned my radio into approximately 700 kHz, left the tape running, and went across the road to the pub. When I came back half an hour later and played back the tape I was amazed to hear a feminine voice, right at the end, calling my name "Norval!" If I hadn't such an unusual name I would have dismissed it as imagination, but apart from the 'v' being rather muffled, it was definitely there.

'At the end of August the Philips tape recorder arrived from Germany and I tried again. When I transcribed the tape I could hardly believe my ears. I'd had the radio tuned in near an Arab station and breaking through the background mush I clearly heard Valerie's voice calling "Norval – Norval! is David (son) in at the start? How are you coping?" I knew it was Valerie. I know her accent, her way of speaking. And my name is so unusual. Also she used the same word I'd used to her before she died – 'coping' – when I mentioned to her about my not being able to cope. I don't know what the reference to David means, unless she's asking if David is involved with me in trying to make contact with her. Needless to say, I was absolutely elated. David heard the tape and agreed it's his mother. I set up my recording equipment every evening at 10.30 pm, went across to the pub, came back and transcribed the tape. At the beginning of October, a female voice broke through the static speaking very fast. She obviously had Valerie with her as I heard her voice in the background. The voices were very mechanical and seemed to be produced on a modulated radio wave band. They were hard to follow. I did pick out some sentences and I had the impression the female speaker was a helper of some kind teaching my wife how to make better contact. Again I recognised Valerie's voice.

'In November, I put a message on a note-pad for Valerie telling her I loved her and left it by the pillow in our bedroom. About the middle of that month I received a letter from my friends in Germany telling me they'd had a letter from Manfred, the EVP researcher. He doesn't speak English but he had told my friends that he'd had a communication for me which read: "Nori (my nickname) has written on note-paper. Manfred – Nori – Understand. Here stands Valerie." I was quite overwhelmed by this. Obviously she couldn't get through to me on that occasion, so she contacted Manfred.

'November was a good month for me because on the 24th I received the longest message so far from my wife. When I came back from the pub I found seventeen minutes of speech on the tape. The name "Valerie" and "Val" is mentioned twenty-one times. Valerie's voice says at one point "Norval, liar. But I love him." This is a reference to the fact that I always used to tell her that I loved her and she would say, teasingly, "You're a liar." She also says "Norval, Babby, love" (I used to call her Babby), and there are three phrases beginning "Unaccepted" and ending "Poor, poor Valerie" plus a lot of female voices in the background apparently coaxing her to speak.

'I can tell you I was one of the world's greatest sceptics before Valerie died, but I am now utterly convinced, without a shadow of doubt, that my dead wife isn't dead in the sense we think of it. She has spoken to me from the other side and I know now there is life after death. I have had one more piece of evidence of survival. In one of my early messages to Valerie I asked her to knock twice if she was here. At about 3am on the morning of the 3rd October I was awakened by a loud bang at the foot of the bed where my tape recorder and radio are. I got up startled and said "Is that you Valerie?" Then there was another loud bang. At about 8.30am I got a phone call from England that her brother John had passed away in the early hours of the morning.'

Norval brought his tapes of Valerie's discarnate voice along and I listened to them. It is usually very hard indeed to listen to a recording of paranormal voices especially if it is not yours. To begin with, a very different method of listening is needed. One has to listen 'through' the noise. There's always a background noise even if a radio hasn't been used to provide a carrier wave for the voices to modulate. This is produced by the recording head and the electrical field always present. The voices themselves can be curiously flat and one-dimensional. And of course the voices and the information are very subjective. The speaker may have been known to the recipient who would be familiar with tone, accent, intonation and content, making what is said easier to decipher. Also the very fact of not having been present at the time of recording seems to distance another listener from the impact of someone else's discarnate voices. It's almost comparable to having to look through someone else's holiday snaps. You shuffle through them as quickly as possible feeling relatively bored and detached. Having said that, in Norval's case, the trial of listening to his tapes was minimal as the voices he described he heard were distinctly audible to me as well especially the 'Norval – Norval! Is David in at the start? How are you coping?'

I had invited Douglas to dinner along with Norval that evening. Vic was there too so that made four of us. Douglas did his automatic writing and after dinner got a message from Paul which said 'Letter in the post for Victor. Yes

– his job.' Vic had been having a difficult time getting work in the past few weeks, so he was pleased to hear he'd be getting some offers. Norval placed his Philips tape recorder in the middle of the table and asked Valerie to knock twice if she was present. The four of us left the table and moved to another part of the room to sit round the fire. We were talking about things in general and Valerie in particular when there were two enormously loud bangs from Norval's recorder. They were so loud, we nearly jumped out of our skins and thought something had fallen from the ceiling onto the table and that if it had hit the recorder, it must be broken. Nothing whatsoever had fallen and we all agreed there was no way anything could have caused those knocks other than an unseen force. So was Valerie at dinner too? Perhaps I should have laid a place for her. A final postscript to this evening was that two days later Vic received an offer of a job through the post.

Up to this point we had tried to get EVP voices using only a tape recorder with inbuilt mike, apart from the one attempt using radio 'mush' when the man's voice gave me some numbers for the lottery – or I interpreted the sounds I heard as numbers. It was difficult to go back on that one and check as I wasn't recording at the time, not really expecting anything to happen. As my Aiwa micro-cassette recorder had finally given up the ghost, I'd laid it to rest in a drawer against the day when I could find someone to miraculously repair its delicate, intricate circuitry. No-one had been able, or willing, to make it work again, probably because it was more expedient not to in order that I should have to buy another recorder, which I did. I bought an Olympus Pearlcorder micro-cassette but from the beginning it didn't hold a candle to the old Aiwa. Anyhow, I thought I'd have another try at recording for EVP using a radio. I used Airband at 125 MHz (the mush) and the Olympus. 'Speak to me please,' I said. 'Anybody, please speak to me.' I heard a muffled, whooshing sound from the radio and then, incredibly, a man's wobbly voice, rising and falling on the sound wave, said: 'Do you want me to come through?' I nearly fell over but managed to gasp out 'Oh, yes — oh, yes! please please speak to me.' But he said no more. This time I'd been recording. I hastily re-wound the tape and listened. There it was, quite distinctly: 'Do you want me to come through?' Why, oh why didn't he?

George Bonner says that although he records sentences of normal length and correct grammatical construction, very few follow on to a conversation. 'Most are brief interludes giving brief information, often incomplete.' He quotes as examples a male voice which states: 'We are farmers in this place' and 'Bonner is quite a healer … never sorry'. 'What exactly is being farmed – and where is the place? or could it be an allegorical comment? What is meant by "never sorry"? Was it part of the last statement or a new remark not fully recorded?' A pleasant female voice told him, 'We have beautiful news for you,' but never went on to explain what that news was. Bonner debates whether the existence of the voices and their survival implications is the beautiful news. These tantalising comments consisting of one or a very few words were beginning to be familiar to me now, fitting in with the man who asked: 'Do you want me to come through?' and then said no more.

Bonner also describes how, during a very late night recording session, he fell asleep on the sofa, sliding to the floor in a half sitting, half lying position. Two hours later he awoke to discover himself in this awkward pose, feeling very stiff. His recording equipment was still running, but he wasn't in the mood to listen to the playback and left it until the following day. When he did listen through the evening's recording, he heard a number of whispered male and female voices discussing him amongst themselves, but was astonished to hear, as well, the crystal clear voice of a young, intelligent and cultured female say: 'Bonner looks quite ridiculous!' Whilst recording and falling asleep on the sofa on another occasion, he captured voices which said: 'Bonner's laying on the settee asleep' and 'Let's visit him while he's asleep.'

One evening I recorded alone in the back room. Vic was away somewhere and only Gorbie, our Siamese cat who had been a little tower of strength during the days after Paul's death, was in the room with me. I was using the Olympus recorder and a new Panasonic tape. I had to go and get something in the cellar, so I left Gorbie in the room alone while I went through the kitchen and down the wooden steps to the cellar. Before I left the room I patted Gorbie and said to him: 'Be a good boy Gorbie-Mannie' (my silly name for him). On playback you hear me talking to the cat, and footsteps going through the kitchen, down the cellar steps, back up again and the sound of me coming back into the room. Then a man's voice, sharp and very quick, says loudly: 'Gorbie -Mannie!' The voice was so fast it needed slowing down to make it comprehensible. On another evening, the 6th of July, after some friends had left, I went into the back room and spoke a few words into the recorder saying I hoped the spirit friends could come through during the period of time I was going to leave the room. When I returned and played the tape back, whistling had been recorded in a completely empty room. It was on a rising scale – a little tune (I checked it out with Vic who is a musician):

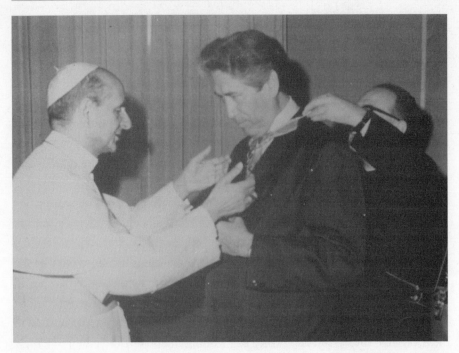

Friedrich Jurgenson being decorated by Archbishop Heim. Photo courtesy of Colin Smythe.

two Gs, two As, then one A sharp. It was not any melody I knew, in fact it was quite eerie. It reminded me of the off-key electronic music from the sci-fi film *Close Encounters of the Third Kind*.

As the weeks went by I learned more about the phenomenon which had helped so much to change my grief and despair into hope. One aspect was intriguing. The relationship of the Catholic Church with the EVP.

On 17 September 1952 Father Pellegrino Maria Ernetti of the Benedictine Order of Venice, a lecturer in prepolyphonic music, stayed late in the laboratory for experimental physics at the Sacro Cuore University in Milan. With him was the famous physician Dr. Father Agostino Gemelli. The two Fathers were making oscillographic experiments with a wire magnetophone. Every time something went wrong, Father Gemelli implored his dead father, 'Help me daddy!' When their experiments ended, they listened to what had registered on the magnetophone. To their utmost surprise, they heard a voice saying: 'I am always with you and help you!' Father Gemelli recognised the voice of his dead father, and the two Fathers listened over and over again to his words, hardly able to believe their ears. Then Father Gemelli said to the magnetophone: 'Daddy, if you are really here, please repeat what you said before.' The answer came like a flash: 'Yes, it's me. Don't you recognise me, my Testone?' (Testone means a pig-headed obstinate person and was the pet name the father had given to his son).

Pope Pius XII, informed of the Fathers' direct communication from the spirit world, reassured them they had no need to worry as the existence of the voice they recorded was a scientific fact and had no basis in spiritism. Father Pistone, Superior of the Society of St. Paul in England, stated: 'What we are faced with is a phenomenon; we need accept no more and can accept no less.'

The Vatican seems to have shown a great deal of off-the-record interest in the EVP and some distinguished Catholic priest-scientists have conducted experiments of their own. The late Professor Gebhard Frei, an internationally recognised expert in the field of depth psychology, was pre-eminent amongst these in the 1960s. He was a cousin of the late Pope Paul VI who in 1969 decorated Friedrich Jurgenson with the Commander Cross of the Order of St. Gregory the Great. This was ostensibly for documentary film work on the Vatican and Pompeii. Jurgenson was deeply interested in Pompeii. His first dialogue voices were recorded there in 1967 with, he claimed, his longest uninterrupted recorded conversation lasting twenty-four minutes in which he was able to talk with several close friends who had already passed on. In 1971 he told Peter Bander, a colleague of Colin Smythe, that he had found a sympathetic ear for the voice phenomenon in the Vatican.

I was so interested in the fact that the Catholic Church had proved to its own satisfaction the existence of the EVP as early as the 1950s, yet to my knowledge no statement to this effect had ever been issued, that I wrote a letter enclosing the photocopied information I had on the subject to Cardinal Hume, head of the Catholic Church in England. I received an immediate response, from his secretary. The letter stated: 'Cardinal Hume is out of London at present and has asked me to deal with all correspondence in his absence. I write to acknowledge your letter with enclosures and to thank you for them. With kindest regards.' And that was that. I never heard from the Cardinal. To tell the truth I never expected to. I think that an acknowledgment by the Church of the discovery that the dead could speak to us would rock the foundations upon which the Church is built; a blind acceptance of the status quo as defined at the Council of Nicaea in AD 325. It was at Nicene, a town in Asia Minor, that the Catholic Christian religion was invented.

I had another look at what Michael Roll had to say. Michael, who had formed The Campaign for Philosophical Freedom based in his home town of

Bristol, had already sent me some more leaflets. I read through the one entitled: 'Censored in England where the Church and State is Established'. In the
light of what I had learned about the Catholic Church and its involvement
with the EVP, what he wrote was significant. The leaflet began with a quotation from The Reverend Don Cupitt, Dean of Emmanuel College, Cambridge
writing in *The Daily Telegraph*: 'Somehow, everybody just knows that
Christianity is the Church and the Church is a power structure, an apparatus
for limiting freedom in belief and morals'. Roll continues: 'All scholars who
have studied history agree with Dr. John Baker, the Bishop of Salisbury, when
he says there is no hope for the Churches unless they get back to the teach-
ings of Jesus. In other words, ditch the crazy doctrines and dogmas invented
at the infamous Council of Nicaea in AD 325 by men who thought Jerusalem
was the centre of a flat earth with a red hot ball of fire going round it every
day. At this time historians estimate there were over 150 Christian sects killing
each other as hard as they could go. This is the sole reason why Emperor
Constantine called this Council – to formulate one all-embracing (catholic)
religion that everybody must believe or die. It all went desperately wrong
when a man known as St. Paul (Saul of Tarsus) turned an unhistorical
philosopher known as Jesus into the 17th pagan saviour-god known to historians as Christ. All Christians follow this saviour-god called Christ, not a
philosopher named Jesus. Jesus said as he died on the Cross, "This day you
will be with me in Paradise," not "This day you will be resting in the ground
waiting for your god to come and judge you." It was at the Council of Nicaea
that the priests made St. Paul's pagan saviour-god – Christ – the official religion of the whole of the Roman Empire. Don't forget St. Paul never even met
Jesus! "The definition of a Christian is a person who accepts Christ as God,
their Lord and Master. The creator of the Universe" – The Bishop of London
(and every other bishop).'

Yes, the last sentence struck a chord with me. I didn't get much change
from the bishop I met in St. George's Church, Finsbury Park. I suppose I
dared to ask the question, 'Is there really a heaven?' and he possibly felt unable
to tell me: 'Only if you are a Christian and are prepared to rest peacefully in
the ground (or in an urn) – waiting for God to come and judge whether you
are fit to be resurrected.' As this criterion would exclude most of the population of the world, heaven must be a pretty elitist club, by the Church's
reckoning. So it was hardly surprising I didn't receive a reply from Cardinal
Hume. He might have found some difficulty in commenting on the fact that

priests of his faith had contacted the dead by electronic means available to us all. The concept doesn't quite fit in.

There are very few people involved with the EVP in the UK. In 1971 a young chemistry student at Cambridge, David Ellis, obtained a grant under the Pierrot Warwick Scholarship to study Raudive's voice phenomenon. He did not try to record paranormal voices himself, but merely observed the methods of Raudive whom he met in Germany, and those of other researchers. Ray Cass, a prominent researcher, told me Ellis had visited him. Apparently he asked nothing, wasn't interested in Cass' clear and impressive recordings, but simply had lunch and played with the dog. Ellis's book, *The Mediumship of the Tape Recorder*, was a negative appraisal of the phenomenon. The Society for Psychical Research speedily accepted his blinkered views and closed the door on research into the EVP. As a result the electronic voice phenomenon languished in the doldrums, kept alive in the UK by a mere handful of dedicated researchers. Contrast this with Germany where there are five EVP societies with over 3,000 members between them. The largest is the VTF. The USA and Canada have large groups of experimenters. Austria, Holland, France, Italy, Brazil, Russia, all have research organisations set up, some with qualified electronic technicians like the Grosetto group in Italy founded thirty years ago by Marcello Bacci. I made up my mind that, if no-one else was prepared to do it – and it looked that way – I would form the EVP Society that the UK deserved to have. Then I asked myself the question, 'Where do you begin?' Someone up there was listening because an answer popped into my mind: 'T.V. of course!' There was a programme on television called *Schofield's Quest*. Its content was inviting people on the programme who wanted to 'find' something. Their 'quests' ranged from locating the habitats of the great-crested newt to tracing someone last seen serving tea behind the counter of a NAAFI canteen in World War II. Well, I wanted to find something. I wanted to find people interested in the electronic voice phenomenon to form the nucleus of a new society. I wrote to *Schofield's Quest*, and didn't hear a word from them.

In June we had to buy a vehicle. The house in Ireland was up to roof level. By July the roof would be on. We needed to get over there to sort things out and start the work of making it habitable. My heart sank on both counts. Buying a vehicle and making another house habitable. I'd had enough of both. Having something on four wheels in London (other than a pram) has never seemed to me to be sensible when there is more than adequate public transport. But Ireland demanded a vehicle, and a large one. Things had to be taken – furniture and bedding, tools, books, clothes, cats, ourselves: a thousand and one things. So I began to look for a secondhand Renault 'Hi-top Trafic' van. I was mentally fixed on this particular vehicle as we'd had one before and I found it fairly light to handle. Finally I located one, miles away, and persuaded a friend to drive me over there and check it out. He turned out to have less idea than I had about a vehicle's road-worthiness as, having bought it, it heated up like an oven and nearly burst into flames on the way home. I had to have a new radiator and water pump fitted immediately. A few weeks later it began to leak oil and the back doors wouldn't open. I started to hate it. But we were stuck with it. I felt sure it would never make the long journey to the west coast of Ireland laden with all our belongings.

We decided to go on July 17th, but two days before, the van developed the most horrible screeching noise from the engine area. It sounded as if a banshee had been let loose every time I turned on the ignition. I took it to Fred at Angelo's Garage in Richmond Crescent. While he was having a look under the bonnet, I glanced across at No. 1 – the house opposite – thinking how, if I'd paid whatever a house of that size would have cost in the best part of Islington, I wouldn't want to be opposite a garage, when Tony Blair, our future Prime Minister, walked down the front steps into a waiting red car. Stating the obvious, I said to Fred: 'Is that Tony Blair's house?' 'Yes,' he replied. 'Do you do his car?' 'Angelo does,' he replied. The reflected glory didn't do me any good though. The van began to screech again as soon as we turned the corner into our street.

That evening, my birthday, Douglas invited me over to his house. He was giving a little party. He began to do some automatic writing on top of the fridge in the kitchen and said to me: 'I've got Paul here and he's saying "Don't worry about the van. It'll be all right. It's not a major thing." Then he described an oblong belt about eighteen inches long which he'd just seen a picture of clairvoyantly. 'Paul's going to look at the van,' he said, 'but you've got to take it back to the garage.' The astonishing thing is Douglas had no idea I had been to the garage earlier that day, nor that there was any further problem with the van. The earliest I could phone Fred was Monday. I explained the van was still screeching and Fred said: 'Get an alternator belt for it.' So the van did need a belt, just as Douglas had said. And it looked as if Paul was going to keep an eye on us.

I was very happy about that. It's a long journey and I was dreading it. We had to change the date of going to Ireland to the 19th. But when we arrived the sun was shining. The view out over the mountains with sea to the left and forest all around was breathtaking. Neither of us had been to Ireland for twelve years, we'd forgotten how beautiful it is. And in the middle of a building site strewn with oil cans, broken roof slates, bits of plastic pipe and breeze blocks, stood our house.

After the euphoria of breathing fresh air for the first time in months and drinking in scenery straight out of *The Sound of Music*, it suddenly registered that we'd come for three months to live in a grey, echoing barrack-like shell that looked like something left over from the last war. There was no electricity and the only water was in the stream running along the top of the land. We walked from room to room. There weren't even any doors. Rubble and concrete dust was everywhere. The walls were unplastered, the windows had a two-inch gap all round them. There weren't any ceilings. We looked up into the rafters – and saw Bug, one of the cats we had brought with us. He glared down at us with furious yellow eyes. We tried to coax him out but he just ran off along the cross beams and disappeared into the eaves. The next glimpse we had of him was his head sticking out from a hole under the roof barge boards. He stayed up there for a week.

The next day Vic built a furnace on ground near the house. It was made of abandoned breeze blocks and worked beautifully. He got a roaring fire going inside it – sparks flew everywhere and tongues of flame leapt out of the gaps between the blocks. We washed out an old metal drum we found, hoisted it on top of the chimney and filled it with water. It heated in no time and we could wash ourselves. As there was an endless supply of twigs from the four acres surrounding the house, the furnace also boiled water for tea, fried eggs and bacon, and gave us lots of hot water to wash ourselves and our clothes. We were camping in a concrete tent. Three weeks later the men from the electricity board came to start installing our supply.

When we lived in Ireland years before, Paul and Vic had erected a wooden shed on ground that was above the old house we had, but was now below the new one, near to a tributary of the Glengarriff River that divided our land from the land we formerly owned. One blazing hot day we carved out a path through waist-high grasses, gorse bushes and wild rhododendrons to reach the spot where the shed had stood. The area was unrecognisable. Before we'd left, twelve years ago, hundreds of trees were planted on this upper ground which had been bare mountainside, other than for gorse and rhododendrons. They were little spindly things – beech, ash, pines, eucalyptus. Now they were massive. Some forty feet high and more. We simply couldn't orientate ourselves. The view was different. Everything was different.

More by chance than planning we stumbled on the shed. It was now in a jungle – dark and impenetrable. Even the course of the river which had been near it had changed. It was running underneath the shed's floor, flowing round the foundation blocks. Spiders scampered as we creaked the door open, ivy tendrils exploring the dark, secret interior, curled from the ceiling. Incredibly, the shed was dry except for a doormat which had become home for a vivid green carpet of moss. Two chairs, a television aerial, a pan and two mugs were still inside. The chairs were rush-bottomed – or had been when we last saw them. Some creature had enjoyed many meals of them. It was so sad to stand inside and remember the day when this little wooden building had been delivered, flat in boxes, and the two brothers had linked the pieces together, heaving up the roof, fixing on the door which now hung so forlornly by one rusty hinge. We decided to dismantle the shed and bring it up near the house. It deserved a new home. When the builders returned to finish levelling off the site round the house with a digger we asked them to dig out a pond in marshy land near the house. They looked at us as if we were mad. Why should anyone want a pond in a country traditionally full of water? They did it nevertheless. A huge muddy hole appeared. It suited the house – a war-torn house and a bomb crater. Gradually it filled with cloudy water seeping out of the churned up blue clay land. It was hard to imagine this enormous puddle would ever contain crystal clear water, lilies and drag-onflies. Looking around, it was very hard to believe the grey barracks in its ravaged setting could ever be made homely; that grass would ever grow and birds – who were noticeably absent – would ever sing around the place again. Still, the view was wonderful, the sky was blue, the air was fresh, and Bug had come down from the rafters. We started work.

I was still thinking about starting an EVP society so I wrote to *Schofield's Quest* again, as though I hadn't written before, giving them a résumé of the phenomenon and why I wanted to be on the programme. This time I had a reply. They asked if I would be in London on September 18th and if so, would I come along to the offices of London Weekend Television and meet one of the researchers? I wrote back saying I would be in London on that date and I would be happy to meet him. On September 13th I returned to London by coach. The house looked lonely, but wonderfully comfortable, especially after the barracks. The red light on the answering machine was blinking. The tape was full. I listened to it. I hadn't realised so many people didn't know we weren't there. I went into the garden. Everything had wrapped itself round everything else. It was a riot, after such a short time. The brick patio had almost disappeared under a carpet of grass and dandelions. The grass would have to go but I like dandelions so maybe they could stay. One huge velvety Deep Secret rose bowed its head forward through a mass of virginia creeper which I'd never planted. It had infiltrated from someone else's place. The Paul's Scarlet rambler had extended some fingers onto the roof of the shed. I thought of 'the mound' and Mick the Plasterer. It was only three years, but it seemed so long ago. I looked up at my bedroom window. My eyes blurred with tears. 'Oh, Paul. I miss you so much!' That night I dreamed of Paul. He was wearing a bright red sweater (a colour he never wore). We were in a run-down house which we were intending to do up. I went over to him and put my arms round him and said, 'I love you so much'. He or I (I don't remember who) said: 'We must have known each other all our lives – all our other lives.'

I invited Douglas over to dinner the following evening. Earlier I'd written a letter to a friend in Germany telling her about my appointment with the researcher at London Weekend Television, and my hopes about being able to get the EVP Society going. I'd added to the letter, 'But there's many a slip twixt cup and lip' – and then had to explain what that meant as her English wasn't quite up to old maxims. We had dinner, and then Douglas did his automatic writing. He said Paul had come through to him. I asked him to ask Paul if *Schofield's Quest* would include me in its programming. Douglas wrote the answer. It was: 'Yes, probably – but there's many a slip!'

As it turned out, there weren't any slips. I went to the LWT offices and met the researcher and the producer, gave as brief a résumé of the EVP as possible, illustrated by one of Ray Cass' voice tapes (which were more audible than mine at that stage of my research) and they said I would be included in the live transmission on October 22.

On returning home I had a nice surprise. A letter had arrived for me from an insurance company with a cheque for £400. It was redemption on a policy I'd cancelled just before leaving for Ireland. This cash in hand, or as good as, revived an idea I'd had coming to London on the coach. I would buy a secondhand car, drive back to Ireland, leave the car over there for use the following year and we'd return to London in the van and sell it. The thought is father of the deed, so I immediately crossed the road to the newsagents, bought *Loot* (the bible of people who are buying or selling something in London) and looked through the Volkswagen section. Helmut, in Ireland, had an ancient VW Polo which was still running, so that's the car I looked for. Right at the bottom of the column of Golfs, Passats, Sciroccos and Polos I saw it: 'Metallic blue Polo LX 1982: Lady owner £330'. The colour appealed to me. I knew that was the one. The following day a blue VW Polo with a large dent in the side and half a million miles on the clock stood outside my house. I liked it immediately. Cars, like people, have personalities, or maybe the people who've used them have imbued them with their vibrations. I didn't like the van at all, but I knew this little blue car would look after me and get me safely back to Ireland. When I started cleaning it I found a yellow Metropolitan Police 'Illegally Parked' ticket stuck to the inside of the spare tyre cover. It was dated 26 August 1992 (the day Paul started to die) and stated: 'This vehicle has been authorised for removal'. Just seeing the date baldly written out like that upset me, but at the same time I thought it was a curious synchronicity.

Two days later I set off back to Ireland giving myself ten hours in which to do a five hour journey to Swansea. The car went like a bird and I arrived in Swansea with four hours to wait for the ferry. I felt that was a bonus. I'd survived the motorway; I was going back home. Curiously enough the barracks felt more like home now than the house in London. Next day Cork looked beautiful as it sailed into view. Rows of little picture-book buildings in colour-washed blues, ochres and pinks against a background of emerald green quilted hills. The roads to the west were quiet, the atmosphere tranquil. It began to rain gently, it was good to be back. For the first time since Paul died I felt optimistic that things could only get better.

Ireland and back again

Butterflies everywhere – red admirals. They flew in as Vic opened the front door of the barracks when I got back. Dozens were already inside, silently gliding round the rafters, dreamily fluttering against window panes. As we opened the windows to let them out, more flew in. It reminded me of a film I'd seen ages ago where Elizabeth Taylor and (probably) Richard Burton built a house in the path of an ancient elephant walk in Ceylon. The elephants tolerated it for some months, then suddenly one day formed a massive herd and trampled their way through the house to regain their ancestral right of way. Perhaps we'd inadvertently built in the path of butterflies. What beautiful creatures they were. We were glad they didn't want to leave; they added a splash of living colour to the interior greyness. Vic told me the builders had called and were intending to start putting ceilings in and plastering the house inside and outside about the middle of October. I told him about *Schofield's Quest* and that I had to be back in England by October 22, so we arranged to leave on the 18th and return the following year. He agreed it was a good idea to leave the Polo under wraps next to the house until we returned. We packed the van with everything we needed to take back. There seemed to be almost as much as we brought – barring furniture.

The morning of departure was bright and sunny after several days of rain. The cats were installed in the van, suitably tranquillised. We got in. I turned the ignition key, put it into first gear, and the van made the most frightful screeching noise as the front wheels span in an ever widening ever deepening trough of mud. Black smoke poured from the engine and we both leaped out. The hateful thing had got its own back after my doubting it would ever bring us to Ireland and foolishly trusting it would take us back. There was nothing for it but to hastily unpack everything, distribute most of the larger items in the house roof space, hoping the builders would remember to cut a loft door in the corridor ceiling so we could get them out again, and decant into the Polo. It was packed to the roof. We left the van in the exact spot from where it had refused to budge. The builders would have to move it.

The day after we returned to London Vic got a job on the new British

Library as a senior electrical technician on a contract. Everyone had contracts now and had to be self-employed.

Schofield's Quest was on Sunday. I had my hair done on Saturday. After weeks of washing it in the stream in Ireland, it looked like a bird's nest. A car came to pick me up on Sunday to take me to the studio. It was a live programme, so the rehearsal went on all day. The researcher had asked me to bring a photograph of Paul to show on screen. I chose one I knew he would have approved of. He was looking his best, smiling that crooked smile he had, sitting beside one of his past girlfriends whose name I'd forgotten. I know the man who started the show off was something to do with model theatres. I don't know what his 'Quest' was. All I can remember is him standing behind a table which had arranged on it those cut-out theatres that have red curtains tied with golden cords and inside, on the stage, little Shakespearian figures on sticks gliding in and out, all made of cardboard. He talked for what seemed like hours. Five or six more people followed him, then it was me. My introduction was fairly facile – 'If you hear some strange whistling and whooshing sounds coming out of your radio one night, don't be frightened. It may be people from another world trying to contact you.'

I'd already given them Ray Cass' tape and they'd chosen the worst example to use on the programme. Worst in the sense that, although the story behind the EVP voice he received was interesting, it didn't reproduce well on transmission. It was a voice he recorded while he was walking on the beach near his home in Humberside. He bent to pick up a piece of old, blackened wood near the edge of the sea. It looked as if it had come off a ship and he said to himself, thoughtfully, 'I wonder where this has come from?' Then he put it in his pocket. When he played the tape back there was an answer: one word – 'Hector!' Ray checked records and discovered a ship of this name had sunk off that coastline in the last century. Although a fascinating story, the one word 'Hector' as an example of the EVP wasn't very convincing for an audience who would know nothing about the phenomenon, and also, as it was spoken very rapidly, would probably miss it altogether. I should have deleted it from the tape before giving it to the researcher. Ray's tape contained much better, longer and clearer examples. However, they'd chosen it, so I had to stick with it.

The introduction to my bit related to Paul and the fact that his voice had been recorded via the EVP two years after he died. I did my best in the apparent five minutes allotted me to put across as much as possible about

'Hector' in particular and the EVP in general. I realised as I was talking that it was an impossibility. The phenomenon is so unknown, so startling in its implications, that one needs days, weeks, to convey information about it in any comprehensible and meaningful form. At the end, Philip Schofield, the host on the show, asked me what my 'Quest' was. I said: 'To find people who are interested in, or experimenting with, the EVP. I would like them to contact me.' The camera swung away from me to a bank of telephones and operators: 'Yes, thank you Judith! Will anyone interested in the electronic voice phenomenon ring this special number.'

The next person was already sitting on the pink sofa, cameras on him. That was it! A week later the researcher phoned me and said he had a stack of letters, phone numbers and cassettes for me. They'd all been sent in to the production office. He said he'd send them over by parcel post. When they arrived I searched through the box eagerly. It was so exciting to pull out letters from all over the country relating personal experience of intervention by the phenomenon onto tape recordings.

One fascinating story (and cassette to back it up)was from a married couple in Wales who recorded Simon and Garfunkel's song *Bridge Over Troubled Waters* from the radio. When they played it back, they were amazed to hear, on two separate sections of the song, the sound of children's voices chanting a small section of the lyrics, in a playful, joyous way, almost as if they were dancing round. They wrote that they had absolutely no idea how these children's voices got onto the recording. When I listened to their tape I thought it might be the children of Aberfan in Wales, victims of the coal tip that slid onto their school in the 1960s.

Another person, a professional musician from Essex, wrote that his grandma used to play the piano with him. She died a long time ago. Recently he had been playing the piano and recording himself. When he played the tape back, another pair of hands was playing with him. Many people had simply heard another voice speak one or two words on a recording they were making, often the voice of someone they knew who had died. When I had finally emptied the box, read all the letters, listened to the cassettes they sent, absorbed the brief messages that had been phoned in to the programme, I knew I had the nucleus of an EVP society for the UK.

The cash situation became desperate in December. I'd been out of the workplace so long, I'd lost contact with media people years ago, was computer illiterate and had received no replies from my 'voice-over' attempts.

Then Gorbie got ill. He began to cough occasionally, and there was a hard area in his throat. I took him to a vet who charged a fortune which I had to put on a credit card, but Gorbie didn't get better. He didn't seem to get worse either. I hoped for the best and in the meantime pawned my jewellery. I'd never been into a pawnbroker's in my life and felt degraded and ashamed, although I rationalised the situation. It had arisen because the two houses had cost far more than I had anticipated. The cash flow had all been one way – out. But at least we had two houses well on the way to being paid for, and no mortgages. All Vic's earnings during this period went on keeping us afloat.

Christmas again. We went to Douglas's. It was a disaster. His gas oven wasn't heating to the right temperature and the turkey took ten hours to cook. In the meantime the kitchen filled up with people, two of whom stationed themselves in front of the cooker oblivious to the fact I was trying to make a Christmas dinner – they'd had theirs. Gorbie had taken a turn for the worse. We'd left him at home wrapped up in a blanket as the central heating hadn't been working properly. I was worried about him. He was more than just a cat. He was my stalwart friend of nine years. On this Christmas Day, I had one of my migraine headaches and the turkey, when it emerged, looked revolting. It was limp and pallid. We ate it unenthusiastically. Douglas said he had Paul through by his automatic writing. He asked if Paul ever used the word 'OK'. I looked at Douglas strangely. 'Everyone uses the word "OK",' I thought. 'So what?' But this seemingly irrelevant little word made a lot of sense in the new year that was just six days away.

On Boxing Day, at 2 o'clock in the morning, Gorbie seemed to be dying. He was gasping for breath and we rushed him to a vet we found in Yellow Pages. The vet said he would have to operate on his throat which was almost completely closed by a growth. He took a biopsy to send away. We had to leave Gorbie with him. I wrote a note in my diary on New Year's Day 1996: 'Got up late. Last night was flat – no parties, no cars sounding their horns, no jollity of any kind. Went into bathroom – what was there? A red admiral butterfly. In mid-winter! Gorbie is still at vet's, God knows how we'll pay the bill, it's going to be over £600.'

On January 10th I was invited to take part in a recording of the BBC's *Esther Rantzen Show* and, on the same day, a late-night programme for Live TV in Docklands. The BBC asked me to be ready for the car to pick me up at 4.15pm and we arrived at the studio in Wembley at 5.15. I recognised one or two faces in the hospitality area. Our slot was 'Life after Death' and it was fairly obvious, from the assembled crowd of people milling around excitedly, who else was going to be part of it. I noted 'the religious sceptic' – an earnest middle-aged man with a tweed jacket and pocket bible, 'the new age person' smelling of joss sticks, 'the intellectual' – he just looked it, and Betty Palko, Princess Diana's ex-medium who didn't recognise me. But who was the frighteningly energetic little grey-haired lady who kept creaking up from her seat and touching her toes? I kept hearing her say 'I'm ninety-two' to anyone who looked at her. And there was an elderly man wearing a kilt and roller blades, together with a woman of about seventy-five in a belly-dancer's outfit. I asked her what show she was on. '*Golden Oldies*,' she replied joyously. So, there we all were – the 'Life after Death' crowd and the 'Golden Oldies' – a symbiotic coupling and captive audience for each other's shows. Two for the price of one for the production company.

Several hours later we, the 'Life after Death' contingent, were still waiting around. The other lot went into the recording studio first. Some of us watched on monitors as one woman of seventy-five who'd had two hip replacements cheerfully chattered on about how she loved abseiling off church towers while another, wearing a silver pants suit with an armful of plastic flowers, confessed with glee she was the oldest disco dancer in town. The old gent with the kilt and roller blades was invited by Esther to take a twirl round the studio and promptly fell over the lighting cables. But it was all good, harmless fun. The man with the tweed jacket and bible cornered me and lectured for fifteen minutes on the wickedness of consorting with mediums and diviners – Deuteronomy, I think, the print was too small for me to read. I asked him why he was against spiritualism as I couldn't see any incompatibility between it and religion – after all Jesus became a spirit. He replied that it was bad for the children to talk about ghosts and spirits – it frightens them. I said I thought violent videos and not talking to the children at all was far more damaging. I hoped we would be able to have this confrontation again in the studio, before the cameras. Time dragged on. I didn't remind Betty Palko of the prediction she made two years ago when she said Prince Charles and Diana would be back together again; instead, we agreed it looked like it was going to be a waste of time coming here.

Finally, at 9 pm, it was our turn. 'Sorry! We're running a bit late. Cameras, lights, applause!' Esther Rantzen, who'd changed her clothes, presumably to make it look as if the two shows were recorded on different dates, bounded in. Some people were already seated on a podium. I recognised only one of them – James Byrne, the medium whom I'd seen perform in Leeds. He had been charged with attempting to get 'messages' for a certain section of the audience, but definitely not for the other section – the sceptics. James tried to explain that messages from spirit didn't come to order and that maybe one would arrive for someone who didn't want it, but he was ignored. Katy Boyle a veteran TV celebrity, was strategically placed in the audience in the section for those wanting messages from James Byrne. She was obviously marked out for a starring role as I'd noticed her having more make-up applied earlier and chatting easily with the crew. We were told to stand up if we wanted to say something when the action started and speak loudly, or we'd be overlooked. This was rehearsed. Then it began.

Esther Rantzen ran in again, to cheering and applause. A lady on the podium was asked to speak first and she rambled on about her father and brother in spirit who warned her of her husband's infidelity. Then Katy Boyle leaped to her feet. The cameras swung round on her. 'It's evil!' she exclaimed. 'Spirits wouldn't get involved in interfering with someone's marriage.' 'A sceptic,' I thought. 'She's in the wrong section.' Then she launched into a convoluted account of how her late husband Grenville always helps her to find parking places whenever she can't find somewhere to park her car. So, was she for or against? It wasn't clear. I looked at my watch. It was 9.28. A car was booked to take me to Live TV at 9.30 to arrive for 10.30. Docklands is just about as far away from Wembley as you can get in London. Fortunately, the cameras were fixed for what looked like it would be the rest of the show on Katy Boyle. I crept out of the back of the studio.

On Live TV they sat me on a red sofa. I was wearing a red dress and shoes, and I have red hair. I managed to talk about the EVP for a few minutes. At least they were running to time and only doing one show. The researchers sent me a video of the programme a week later. I never looked at it, I daren't. I think my bit must look like a clip from a Dracula movie – all that blood on the sofa! Later I read in the cable programme listings they called the slot I was on *Weird Half Hour*.

The biopsy on Gorbie showed he had a slow growing cancer of the larynx. On January 18 he was obviously having great difficulty in breathing so Vic and I took him to the vet for his last chance – an operation to remove the larynx and connect his oesophagus to his chest. We both knew it was hopeless, yet we couldn't watch him struggle to breathe and we couldn't have him put down. As the vet took him away, I looked into his blue eyes, and knew I wouldn't see him alive again. I said to Vic I thought he'd survive the opera-tion but I couldn't see any further than that. We phoned the vet the next day. He said Gorbie had come through the operation and had even had the strength and will to pull out his nasal tube. I was so happy I bought a bottle of Warre's Port to celebrate. The next day they said he was 'not too bad' and would I like to visit him? This sounded like the things they say about people in hospital – a roundabout way of telling you it's your last chance to see them alive. I asked if he was all right, and the receptionist said he was sitting up. I thought it better not to go and see him as he'd want to be taken home and I wouldn't be able to do that just yet. I phoned the next morning at 9 am, and they told me Gorbie had died at 6 am. I was heartbroken. I'd lost a loved and loving friend.

The vet's final bill was over £1,000. I looked round for things to sell. I advertised a stack of quarry tiles that had stood in the cellar since Paul died. A man and his wife came round and bought them for the kitchen of an old house in the country. The boiler that had been in the kitchen before being replaced sold quite quickly, and an antique table. Then, of course, there was the van. But the van was in Ireland. I phoned Helmut and asked him if he knew someone who could bring it over. He said he'd think about it. A couple of days later he phoned back and said he did – Dave, a friend of a friend who wanted to visit his mother outside London. If I paid his fare, he would do it.

I had to have another Siamese cat. I missed Gorbie so much I thought the best thing to do would be to transfer the affection to another Siamese straight away. They are very special cats, almost dog-like. I phoned the Siamese Cat Club to find out if they had an adult male who needed a home. Surprisingly, Annette, the lady I spoke to, said she had one. His owners had just had a new baby, and they had also bought a kitten. Marnine Sims, aged five with a pedi-gree as long as your arm, was jealous of both and destroying the furniture. I immediately said I'd have him. When they brought him to the house he and I came to an immediate understanding. He was exactly the same colour as Gorbie – dark chocolate face, back and paws, creamy chest. He had deep-set amethyst-blue eyes, big ears and a great deal of dignity. He slipped silently from his cage in the sitting room and stationed himself behind the curtains. He didn't emerge until his former owners had left. Then he positioned himself on top of the armchair backrest next to the radiator. He didn't say a word, just looked. I think the other cats thought he was Gorbie reincarnated. They didn't react to him, just accepted him. But he was different. A diamond shaped face, long, narrow eyes and flat bat-like ears – a mysterious air: a lovable alien. I re-named him E.T.

The van was a huge headache. I put another advert in *Loot* and, amazingly, had a phone call from a man who offered me £1,000 without seeing it, but £650 less than I'd asked for. I got him to agree to £1,300 and he said he'd come and look at it. I didn't think he would, but he did, with another man. They walked round it, viewing it from every angle, checking underneath, conferring with each other when I was at the front end and they at the back, and vice versa. I kept my fingers crossed. The driver climbed into the driving seat, I got in next to him. The other man sat at the back. We managed to lurch forward and drive round the block in a kangaroo sort of fashion. Finally, we went back to the house. I thought they'd say they didn't want it, but surprisingly they offered £950. I said, with a loser's desperation, 'Oh, you may as well give me the £1,000 you offered at first; what difference does £50 make?' They conferred with each other at the far end of the sitting room in lowered voices. 'OK!' they said, 'we'll have it,' and counted out the notes. I tried not to grab them with indecent haste. I watched them from out of the window go down the road towards the van. What on earth did they want it for? I clutched the small bundle of new notes tightly. I was so relieved the that our pressing money problems were marginally relieved.

Jupiter, apparently a very damaging planet astrologically, was 'moving out of Cancer at the beginning of 1996', I read, and 'it would be a great year' for me. It hadn't begun very well. January was a write-off for a start. I had done very little recording for the EVP for one reason or another, and not too much writing either. The house, at least, was finished. It looked wonderful. It represented nearly four years of hard work, a great deal of it overshadowed by Paul's death and the huge burden of sorrow it had placed upon Vic and me. The burden was a little lighter now. I still missed Paul desperately. I thought of him virtually all the time. If he wasn't at the front of my mind he was in my soul consciousness. But the discovery of the EVP and the astounding evidence from some mediums meant there was a growing hope and belief I would see him again.

In late February a man named John Sutton, an ex-prison officer who, after a swift change of career, had become the medium James Byrne's manager, asked me to take part in a psychic weekend to be held in Prestatyn, Wales. He wanted me to give a talk about the EVP. I hastily wrote a script. Then a friend suggested I do a tape on the EVP. I thought that was a good idea, but I didn't have the facilities and recording studios charge a lot. The same friend had a JVC dubbing tape deck. 'Can I borrow it?' I asked. He had to lend it to me, it was his idea after all.

The day before the psychic weekend was due to begin on Thursday March 7, I set up the equipment in the back room we used for our EVP sittings. It had good light from the french windows and was quiet. The cats were barred. I wanted it to sound as much as possible as if the tape had been recorded in a studio. It couldn't be too amateurish. I was intending to charge for it. I bought a metal tape as the master to record on, assembled my script, which I'd already edited into a suitable form for recording, together with extracts from George Bonner's EVP voice examples and those of Ray Cass which they'd given me permission to use. These were on a different cassette. Everything was going well. I had the headphones on and I was relating into the mike the story of the tetchy old gentleman in spirit who had ticked me off when I asked about the electricity in the house going off all the time, when I heard a jumble of voices in my ears. The tape deck had two drives – the left to record from and the right for the dubbing tape, in this case my metal master. I thought I'd left Bonner's and Cass' cassette by mistake in the left-hand drive and it had switched itself on (or I'd mistakenly activated it), and was thus recording over what I was saying into the master. I stopped the recording, and looked at the left-hand drive. It was empty. No cassette in it. What caused the jumble of voices I heard? I ran my master tape back to the point where I'd said (after talking about the old gent and the electricity): 'Turn your volume down as the background noise is very loud'; then I carried on speaking a few words. After that I mentioned I'd heard something and the recording stopped. At the precise position on tape following the sentence ending '...very loud' a woman's voice with an American accent said, very quickly, but perfectly clearly, 'Can I hear it?' I had inadvertently captured a voice by the EVP whilst recording a tape on the EVP. It was a perfect example of the spontaneity of the phenomenon and I left it on the master tape, grateful to the anonymous woman from the United States who had clearly been listening to my over-long explanation and was briskly reminding me to cut the cackle and play the example I'd been referring to.

The weekend was interesting. The four mediums were from the north of England which is much closer to Prestatyn than London is, and it appeared most of the guests were from that part of the world too. John had arranged a full programme of psychic awareness classes, clairvoyance, psychometry, spiritual healing and meditation. My EVP talk was to be on the last day, Sunday. The weekend guests were divided into four groups and one medium was allotted to each to take them through the two days of development of psychic powers. I joined one of the groups, participated in everything and and thoroughly enjoyed myself.

On Saturday evening I booked a sitting with one of the mediums, Margaret Eccles. I was curious. I wanted confirmation of the existence of a spirit world from someone else who had never met me and who knew nothing whatsoever about my private life. Would she be able to convince me by providing information she could have had no prior access to? John Sutton, the organiser of the weekend, only knew me by name and by what I had written in the paper. I had been scrupulously careful never to mention anything personal, as I always had in mind this would prejudice any evidence I might obtain from mediums in the future. Margaret came up to my room. She began straight away by saying she was going back eighteen months:

'A lot of heartache, pressure; conscious of your mother who is happy to be in the spirit world, free of pain. You're at a crossroads with work. Your mother is talking about a lot of tears, which means you're a strong lady and don't like to show grief in front of others. She's giving the name of Annie connected to great grandma and Stan – Stanley. Through 1995 you've taken three steps forward and five back. That door should have opened and it slammed, but it's been creative and you've gained a lot of knowledge. You spread it out to others and they use it, and it came from you. You attract flies. People tend to draw to you, want to drain you, take blood from you. Too much has been taken from you. You are keeping your own counsel now. Mother's showing me an expensive crystal which when you hold it to the light you feel as though there was a crack in it, like a flaw. It's symbolic. You've been shattered, into a million pieces. More than pain – aching. Taken a long time to get over it. But he's still with you, still in your thoughts. Doesn't have to be a romance. He's still there, but not there. Have you lost a brother to spirit? I wanted to get hold of you and give you a hug. He's had to come down a level – very powerful. He's gentleness and peace. You're in need of lots of love, warmth, tenderness. You've got an aura that's like a coat of armour but you've started to expand materially and spiritually. You've been put in the right place at the right time. They've been watching your money situation. Peter and Paul. Robbing Peter to pay Paul, to pay Paul back to pay Peter. Your mother's talking about two properties. You're at sixes and sevens with two properties. Do you want to rent one? Do you want to sell one? I don't think the other one will be a home to you. Don't let the one you're in go. I'm in your home now, it feels like a home. You've thought: "I'll go to the other one and rent mine," haven't you. That's what I want to happen. Rent yours. Go to the other one. That's when your life gets sorted. It's been a long, hard haul for you. Do you know the name Leslie? Watch where you have communication with Leslie.'

At this point I asked Margaret: 'I wonder if the brother you said had come through really is a brother?'

Margaret said: 'He came back as a brother. Was he a husband or a partner? Oh! I've had a massive heart attack – snap of fingers – gone! Tremendous pain in my chest then, gone. He says: "Tell her it's me. Tell her I'm free of the pain." So unexpected. He's the last one who should have had a heart attack. But he kept a lot from you. He knew there was something wrong. But he says "I'm in a wonderful, wonderful place," and he wants to give you a tremendous amount of love. I must apologise to you because that's when your life got shattered. That's all the colours that were in the crystal. That's when the pain was, the trauma, the grief. He didn't want to worry you so he kept a lot to himself. He is very much around you. Very much with you and still giving you a tremendous, tremendous amount of love. You are still very very important to this man. Still watches over you. He says, "She's not as hard as she makes out."

I said to Margaret: 'Is this man giving you a name?'

Margaret hesitated: 'I've had a Simon, and I've had a Paul. He just said, "If she wants to know my name, tell her it's Paul." Got a bit stroppy with me there. "Tell her Paul!"'

I'm ashamed to say my 'aura like a coat of armour' cracked wide open when she said 'Tell her Paul!' I could feel the tears well up and try as I might I couldn't stop them oozing out and plopping off my chin. After Margaret had gone to her own room, and I'd recovered my composure, I played the recording I'd made of what she'd said. There was only one name which didn't mean anything to me – 'Annie' connected to Great Grandma. I never even knew my grandmother, let alone my great grandmother, so I had no idea what her name, on both sides of the family, was. Also, I knew only one Simon, Simon Forsyth, the former owner of *Psychic World*, and he was still alive – at least I believed so. However, the rest of what Margaret had said was absolutely and completely correct and accurately reflected my life and emotions as they had been since Paul's death, and as they were at this moment in time. Even the claim he was my brother. Paul always told everyone he was my brother rather than my son. The names Margaret gave were totally accurate. Stan – my eldest sister's husband, and Stanley – my Uncle Stanley on my mother's side; both dead. She mentioned Peter: René's Peter, who I had learned only recently had died. And, of course, Paul. She also made remarks attributed to my mother (who died some time ago) about 'two properties' and my debating whether to sell or rent one or the other. This was quite astonishing, because I had in fact been thinking whether to sell the London house or the house in Ireland and had approached an estate agent. But at the same time I had also considered renting one of them, and had made some enquiries about that too. I hadn't mentioned this to anyone, not even Vic. I know I couldn't sit down in front of someone whom I'd never met in my life and knew nothing about and reel off statements to them which were completely meaningful and evidential. I dismiss the Super ESP theory. So what's left? My mother and Paul were speaking to me from another dimension through the medium of Margaret Eccles.

The following day, Sunday, I gave the talk on the EVP which was well received, although most people looked sceptical, and displayed my 'History and Method of the EVP' tapes on a table. Some of them sold. I was happy about that. At the end of my talk, Lesley Shepherd, one of the four mediums leading the 'weekend', headed straight for me and said: 'I've got to tell you. I've had a man with me who kept saying "Paul", "Paul" over and over again.' Margaret Eccles had advised me to 'Watch where you have communication from someone named Leslie.' I had imagined, hearing the spoken word, she meant the male version Leslie, but here was a Lesley telling me Paul was repeating his name over and over to her for my benefit. My excitement at receiving even more proof of the existence of an after-life was tempered by the possibility that Margaret had mentioned the sitting she had with me the previous evening to Lesley. It was unlikely, as I believed the two didn't know each other, but I couldn't preclude it. My innate scepticism, although assuaged, refused to lie down and quietly die.

Then we did a short demonstration of the EVP. John had a battery recorder which he placed on a table. The four mediums and I stood round it and we attempted to communicate via the EVP and be communicated with. John filmed us with a camcorder. The following Saturday he rang me at home. He was very excited and said that on the video he made of us all standing round the tape-recorder on that Sunday, at a point where I'd said: 'Friends, does anyone want to speak to us?' Lesley Shepherd, the medium, who had been sitting with her back to the camera, radiated with a golden glow around her. He said this lasted a few frames and then disappeared. John sent me a copy of the video and I saw the glow round Lesley myself. It was inexplicable. I didn't want to leap to any conclusions, but had to admit it was curious that this occurred a short while after she had told me Paul was speaking to her but regretfully felt I had to leave an open verdict on it.

While I still had the borrowed JVC tape deck, I took the opportunity of using it at a sitting. I set it up with a new tape to record in the usual way. During the recording I heard a 'fuffing' sound coming from the 600 ohms mike which was hanging up in the centre of the room. I wondered whether to cover up the light coming from the tape deck and got a cloth to drape over it, saying to myself: 'That'll do, that's fine.' Towards the end of the tape E.T. managed to get into the room (whatever he wants he gets – he's like that!) I scold him and then laugh. When I listened to this tape through headphones, at the point where I said: 'That'll do, that's fine,' and just behind my voice I heard my father's distinctive voice say my name: 'Judy' (he called me 'Judy', not 'Judith'). I know it was my father because he was Russian and had a certain accent which he never quite lost. Where E.T. got into the room and I scolded him and then laughed, a bizarre comment had been recorded. It was a young man saying: 'Fucking funny!' It was perfectly clear and unmistakable. But what a strange remark to make. Quite aggressive, not at all spiritual. Later I learned from other EVP researchers that this is not uncommon. Voices will often say something slightly distasteful or not quite in the mould one would expect if they're coming from heaven. But I also discovered that just because someone dies, it doesn't mean he or she becomes an angel. People in spirit remain the same as when they were on earth. So that would explain it.

The other strange thing that occurred is that when I'd set the recorder up to play back through the amplifier and loudspeakers, not having touched anything I shouldn't have, the whole section which contained my father's voice calling 'Judy' had disappeared from the tape.

We hadn't been to Douglas's circle for a while; the three months in Ireland had disrupted the routine. He'd got new people to make up the numbers – seven was the optimum. Halfway through April he phoned and asked if I'd like to be the seventh sitter as someone had said they weren't able to come that evening. A couple of the regulars were round the table – Ian and Debbie, and some new people. They told me they'd been regularly visited by a spirit named Dick from Liverpool who had passed in 1908. He had been a chimney sweep. They were playing music at the sittings now, and he had been attracted by hearing the lovely music which had been played at his funeral. They said that Dick always moved the small tray on the table in time to the music. The tray had fluorescent tabs on it so everyone could see the movements in the dark. Once, he had apparently knocked it, when it had some coins on it, onto the floor and when asked by one of the sitters to pick them up and replace them on the tray, had done so. They also said that sometimes chairs vibrated and the whole room seemed to rock. It looked as though things had progressed since the days of the cabbage that smelt like ectoplasm!

I was eager to witness these events. The sitting began in the totally blacked out room with classical music softly playing. When the music played at Dick's funeral started, the tray rose gently from the table and began to sway in time to the music – backwards and forwards, up and down. I carefully swept the air in as wide an arc as possible, but couldn't feel any hand or arm propelling the tray. Tapped messages told us it was Dick and two other spirits were with him. One sitter asked if we could be touched, especially me, as a newcomer to the circle. Soon after this someone else reported he'd been touched on the back of the head. Another person said he'd been touched on the arm. Nothing happened to me. After a while I asked out loud if I could be touched on the throat. The tray continued to sway and was put gently down when the music finished. At that moment I was touched by what felt like two closed fingers. Unfortunately, they touched my breast and not my throat and really startled me. This caused a great deal of hilarity round the table. After a while I was touched in the same area again and then the tray began to gyrate round the small table to the point where it balanced on the edge of it above my knee but didn't fall. I again carefully swept the air but couldn't feel either human or any other agency propelling it. Then the tray was suddenly pushed to the right of me and fell with a crash to the floor. The 'entity' responsible for this was asked politely to pick it up but very loudly rapped out two knocks for 'No!' on the table. When asked if he was doing something else he rapped out 'I will try voice.' We listened with bated breath. After a short while there was a sort of whirring sound which seemed to come off the table to my right (where Ian, whom everyone considered to be the medium, was sitting). Then I heard a straining, wheezing sound. Again, silence. Then the same sound a little louder. Then I heard the word 'Hello' followed by other strained sounds. After a while, the sounds died away. Everyone attributed the attempt at 'direct voice' to my presence and involvement with the EVP.

In all honesty, I didn't know what to make of the evening's events. I still couldn't make up my mind whether or not one of the circle members was stage-managing the phenomena. Nor could I work out, if someone was doing it, why they were or how? You'd have to have cat's eyes to see in the dark, or night vision binoculars. And why should I so mistrust the events at this circle at the same time as knowing, by my own experiences, there was really something out there? It was a dichotomy unresolved to this day.

We still owed the builders in Ireland £3,000 and it seemed that the only way to pay them, and pay for the central heating we'd had installed in the house in London, would be to let it for sufficient time to cover all our debts. I located a reputable estate agent who found us three girls as tenants. We agreed they should rent the house from the middle of May for six months. Paul, speaking through the medium Margaret Eccles, had shown us a way out of our difficulties.

Douglas brought a friend round one evening. Kaarle is Swedish, lives in Germany and teaches Japanese. He also speaks perfect English. He had contacted me some time before by phone enquiring about the EVP in England. It was nice to meet him in person. He had been receiving EVP voices over quite a long period of time; most of them were pleas for help from, he believed, trapped spirits who couldn't find the way to escape this dimension into the spirit world. He wanted to try an experiment in recording with both Douglas and me present as he hadn't been receiving voices for a while and thought two people he considered mediumistic might help. He had a good tape recorder, a Marantz, and we put in a new tape and sat round in the back room. When he spoke into the machine and we heard the playback there was nothing except a grinding noise like troglodytes chewing stones. When I spoke to Paul, asking him if he was there (or here), on playback we heard a man's voice – not Paul's – say 'A breakthrough!' Later in the tape a different voice said abruptly 'Sikorda' (phonetic spelling). We had no idea what this means. The words 'A breakthrough' could have been a reference to Konstantin Raudive's book of the same name and also, I like to think to my intention to form the EVP Society. 'Sikorda' remains a mystery.

Now, I had to do what I'd been putting off – write to all those people interested in the EVP who had contacted *Schofield's Quest* plus all the people who'd written to me asking for the EVP tape, having read an advert in the paper.

There were over three hundred names and addresses. My typewriter was still acting in a very strange manner, its cassette flying from side to side, wheezing and beeping in all the wrong places. It didn't need a service, it had just had one. I couldn't understand it. This erraticism made it very difficult indeed to do any prolonged bursts of typing. I had to wait until the machine felt like it. It would be typing away perfectly normally, and then suddenly the illuminated green 'On' pointer would go off, and it died. I had to abandon my task and do something else, to be summoned to the machine, when it decided to come back to life, by a crash as the cassette hurled itself to the left and then righted itself at the 'commence typing' position. On the day I decided I must begin to write to everybody to tell them about the formation of the EVP and Transcommunication Society of the UK, I switched on the typewriter, hoping for the best. It sprang to life and a row of kisses appeared on the display screen. I pressed the tabulator to clear them but they didn't clear and instead typed themselves out on the paper I'd inserted, preceded by the initials VC (Victor's initials) which hadn't even been up on the screen. There really was a ghost in the machine that day sending his love to Vic when I was doing all the hard work!

On the evening before we left for Ireland we blocked up the cat doors as Bug had definitely twigged what was going on. Later that night Vic called me to the front door. 'Look!' he said pointing over the road to the small grocer's shop diagonally opposite. 'Can you see that face on the blind?' The shop glass front had a brown calico blind inside which covered the whole window. It was quite an extraordinary sight. The way it had fallen when drawn that evening, in crumpled ridges and hollows, had created a huge face of a Red Indian with hooked nose, heavy brows, head dress and all. The eyes appeared to look in our direction. It was a Fortean phenomenon, and one that could only be seen from our angle of vision. We walked a little way up and down the road in front of the shop and it disappeared. Without wishing to be trite we had to admit it was like the drawings you see in psychic and spiritualist circles of the Spirit Guide 'White Eagle'. I hoped he'd come to guide us safely down the motorway.

The big one

What is the mechanism involved in the EVP? Why is it so little known? I can do no better than quote someone who studied the phenomenon for twenty-five years, George Bonner:

'Psychology, which is the study of the human mind, has in recent years been accepted into the scientific hierarchy. It now defends its new position by a firm mechanistic approach to the nature of consciousness and seeks to persuade us through its complex theories that the paranormal exists only in and through our consciousness. Consequently, paranormal phenomena such as the EVP cannot really exist and must be explained away as imagination or projection. This at least is the theory and unfortunately, especially here in the UK, it seems to have been accepted by many without further thought or investigation. Many of those who first showed great interest around 1969 to 1972 in Dr. Raudive's research with the publication of his book *Breakthrough: An Amazing Experiment in Electronic Communication with the Dead* soon shied away from the subject. Doors that had begun to open, closed. The subject was dropped. The implication that the voices were errors of the mind had sunk in and produced their negative effect.

'This incorrect conclusion of a known psychological process made otherwise intelligent people afraid to challenge the theories of psychology, now a part of science. The EVP, at least in Britain, became a casualty of this confused thinking. Only a handful continued to study it or make recordings on a regular basis. Abroad, however, they formed themselves into groups exchanging information and data and working in close co-operation with acoustic and electronic experts. Yearly conferences were arranged, papers published. The EVP was discussed on radio programmes and featured in press reports. Hundreds were involved, while here it was difficult even to get an article on this work published in a popular magazine. True, one or two scientists had begun to take seriously metal bending as a possible psycho-kinetic effect, which of course would still be explained within the mechanistic view of nature; but my efforts to interest university parapsychologists in this country failed to obtain any response. In the climate that exists here perhaps this is not surprising since most of our discoveries seem to find their way abroad. In 1977 I sent a copy of my paranormal voice recordings to the distinguished German parapsychologist Professor Dr. Hans Bender then of Freiburg University. He expressed his interest and remarked upon the clarity of the voices. Later my research information was passed on to Dr. William Braud of the Mind Science Foundation, San Antonio, Texas. Dr. Braud corresponded with me on EVP and in 1981 he lectured in Dallas on the Voice Phenomenon and mentioned my own research and name. This lecture was later issued as a paper. Both the USA and the USSR have, in recent years, shown a keen interest in certain aspects of paranormal research that might have certain military uses and although it is not my intention to consider these implications here, I can hardly believe that this interest in EVP research would have been undertaken in the first place had the psychological theory of projection been taken seriously, and I think that in rejecting the possibility of the reality of the EVP, some parapsychologists in the UK have brainwashed themselves. They are so self-conditioned in their thinking patterns that they are unable to move beyond or even consider, let alone accept, other concepts of reality. This has unfortunately happened in many areas of research, as for example the failure to recognise the great value of hypnotism in medicine in all types of illness including organic disease. It is not really surprising that so little is known about the EVP especially when we remember that only one text book on the subject, *Breakthrough*, has been published here and in America and that back in 1971.

'Let us now consider what we have learned about the essential mechanisms involved in recording EVP and the main characteristics displayed by the voices themselves. Researchers have long suspected that the intelligences behind the voices require certain basic sounds in order to make themselves audible to us. The early Raudive voices were recorded using the radio method tuned to a mixture of white noise on interfrequency. Unfortunately this sound could at times swamp weaker paranormal voices so it is important to obtain the correct signal to noise ratio.

'Certain critics suggested that we were mistaking noise for voices and of course we know that this illusion is possible when we listen at any length to monotonous and repetitive sounds. However voice print tests by spectogram of my recordings made at the Joint Speech Research Unit clearly give objective proof that the voices are human speech. The actual significance of noise to the production of paranormal voices is not clear, although noise produces thermal energy.

'Of course, more recent investigation has suggested that certain frequency combinations can assist the 'metamorphosis' process that is felt to be used in fabrication of EVP. Jurgenson claimed as far back as 1959 that normal radio broadcast material, speech, music or even morse could be changed 'instantly' to produce brief paranormal messages from the dead. Unless one has heard this for oneself it is hard to credit. Obviously in EVP recordings we are involved in a strong energy exchange in which the time factor is also important. The strange characteristic of EVP speech has long been noted and was used by Raudive to differentiate EVP from normal radio intrusion, a process that unfortunately led to some errors in interpretation.

'Most of the early recordings of Jurgenson and Raudive were received in a mixture of different languages. This is called polyglot. On top of this, made-up words or neologisms would be heard; laws of grammar would be murdered and the voices spoke very rapidly, often two or three times faster than normal speech. They also spoke in a peculiar sing-song rhythm. These characteristics noted by all researchers seem to have been accepted without further regard as to their cause. It made correct voice interpretation difficult at times and increased the possibility of error. Most researchers now record voices that speak in their own language, although occasionally words may be received in a mixture of two languages or more. In my opinion this suggests that available material must be used for modulation and that a rigid word economy is observed. This, in effect, produces the telegram style of message so often received with the consequential grammatical errors including the use of neologisms plus other twists to word endings made necessary by the brief duration allowed in transmissions. All these characteristics have, I believe, the purpose of energy conservation. It is also possible that the voice entities make use of different forms of energy, although free energy is available from radio and television transmissions.

'It was once conjectured that the voices might be impressed directly to the magnetic tape by some kind of PK energy and this theory was advanced by those who suggested the origin of the voices was the researcher's own unconscious. Such an idea, if accepted, would of course avoid any necessity to consider the survival hypothesis. However, this is not the case. The tape recorder merely functions in its normal capacity to record and store all information that is fed into it. In the radio interfrequency technique that produces the loudest and clearest voices, these can often be heard as they come over the loudspeaker. Due to the speed of the voices, they often cannot be deciphered without replaying the tape, and slowing them down. Consequently, the EVP would not be spotted in the first place without the tape recorder making this possible.

'Reception of the EVP depends upon paranormal voice modulation of a random frequency or a multi frequency voice band carrier and this we provide on our electronic equipment. Sound of some kind is essential and voices will not be recorded in a vacuum. This sound source can be natural, mechanical or electronic. Some believe the voice entities in the beyond create their own high energy fields via gravitational forces which are able to project through screening and these reveal a directional effect. Jurgenson insisted a carrier wave was essential for recording EVP and further that he had a mediator in the beyond called Lena who told him when to record. He also claimed to record on a specific frequency around 1475kHz on Medium Wave although the only other person I know of personally to make successful recordings on this spot is Luise Fuchs of Allfeld, Germany.

'Veteran British researcher Richard Sheargold (deceased) who had over fifty years experience in the electronics industry and was also an amateur radio ham, believed all the voices were metamorphosed from existing radio material in the radio method or from the myriad of small sounds that impinge upon the microphone using that method. I have been told in my recordings "In truth we go through your radio set" . A curt female voice also stated "Insist on radio". Other voices have also told me "This is a radio contact" and "Tune to this frequency". I have also been told "Use short wave, it's the high frequency".

'Quite apart from the basic electronic techniques used to record EVP I believe the researcher acts as a link or sensitive between two dimensions of existence, therefore our psychological attitude towards this research may well be a vital factor. We are dealing with an active collaboration that is leading us to undiscovered laws that involve the experimenter.'

Before publishing Raudive's book, Colin Smythe set up two carefully controlled experiments in 1971 supervised by Pye Records Ltd. The first of these was on March 24 at Gerrards Cross, Buckinghamshire. The two chief

The experiment conducted by Pye Records in 1971. From left to right: Ronald Maxwell, Dr Konstantin Raudive, Peter Bander and a Pye engineer. Photo courtesy of Colin Smythe.

recording engineers of Pye Records, Ray Prickett and Keith Attwood, supervised the experiment and all the equipment was provided by the record company including instruments to block out freak pick-ups from radio stations and high and low frequency transmitters, as well as specially protected tapes. A bank of four tape recorders was synchronised so that one recording was made through a microphone giving a true account of any normal noises in the room, and a sophisticated diode was also fitted with a recording indicator attached. This machinery was guaranteed to render any recording through the diode impossible. Dr. Raudive was present together with Peter Bander (a colleague of Colin Smythe and at that time, an arch sceptic, who later wrote the preface for the translation of Dr. Raudive's book) and Sir Robert Mayer, Chairman of Colin Smythe Ltd. The tapes ran for 18 minutes during which time the recording indicator attached to the diode flickered constantly, although Ray Prickett, monitoring on headphones, could hear nothing.

Over 200 voices appeared on the tape, 27 of which were so clear they were audible and intelligible to everyone present. Sir Robert Mayer in particular was startled to recognise the voice of his old friend the late Artur Schnabel, a celebrated concert pianist. An unidentified voice referred to Dr. Raudive as 'Kosti' – his childhood nickname.

The second experiment was conducted three days later on March 27 at the Enfield Laboratories of Belling and Lee using a radio-frequency screen laboratory that excludes any type of electromagnetic radiation. The experiment was supervised by Peter Hale, Britain's leading expert in electronic screen suppression. He was assisted by Ralph Lovelock, a top physicist and electronics engineer. Again clear voices appeared on screened-off tapes. Peter Hale's response was frank. 'The result of last Friday's experiment ... is such that I cannot explain it in normal physical terms,' he wrote to Colin Smythe. Ralph Lovelock concurred with this view. So the objective reality of the voices, whatever their cause, was established to the satisfaction of highly respectable scientists.

So, what are the techniques used to record voices by the electronic voice phenomenon?' To quote George Bonner:

'Great care is needed both in listening and in the analysis of recorded material. This requires not only good hearing but also the correct psychological approach. I believe that it is quite possible that paranormal voices have tried to make contact with us since the early days of radio, coming in near to normal radio frequencies, but were either not heard or were dismissed as normal radio intrusion. In the radio method which gives the best results we are also picking up normal radio signals and it takes some experience to know which is radio and which may be paranormal.

'Paranormal voices can display some peculiar characteristics – the polyglot mode, neologisms, the disregard for laws of grammar, the fast speed of the speech and also the peculiar rhythm of the voices, although I believe that since I began recording EVP voices they have changed and are now often indistinguishable from normal speech in their rhythm and speed. One has to learn to recognise these characteristics but even more important, to master the knack whereby we can instantly pick out weak voices by latching onto the one-dimensional tone so we can separate speech from noise and paranormal voices from radio. It can take time, a quick and alert mind and lots of patience to do this correctly. Quite often when I play EVP recordings that to me are quite clear, people unfamiliar with this type of sound will hear nothing except a noise. Repeat the process two or three times and they will suddenly recognise words. Once they realise that EVP can lay hidden and masked in noise or between radio they become alert and able to spot for themselves voices they never knew existed. It took Dr. Raudive three months before he was able to hear his first voice, so be prepared to devote time to this research.

'You may well have recorded paranormal voices but still have failed to hear or identify them on replay. Some may at first just hear a noise, then they isolate this from other noises. They then detect a definite rhythm and depth and by following this are able to differentiate first vowel sounds, then consonants and finally understand words. The mind can only concentrate fully on one voice at a time, so that if we received on tape three voices speaking together, as often happens, it can create to the inexperienced confusion and all be dismissed as 'noise'. With the tape recorder we can repeat this section of the tape and listen to each individual voice. We can then decide what is said by each one and in this manner study the material and on this basis of content decide whether any voices are paranormal. This form of listening requires concentration and freedom from distraction. We cannot carry out this type of research if we are tired or harassed.

Correct interpretation of what we record is essential but even the experts can make mistakes. Jurgenson discovered years ago that even normal radio material can be altered and words twisted to provide a brief message. Thus one minute we may be listening to a normal radio programme when suddenly by some instant metamorphosis words are altered to produce a personal message. Unless one has heard this for oneself it is hard to believe it possible, but one thing we learn early on in EVP research is that the paranormal voices do not obey the (known) laws of electronics or of physics.

One's individual approach to a recording will be influenced to some extent at least by the actual technique used. Here I would like to discuss what is known as the 'Radio Method' sometimes referred to as the interfrequency technique. Raudive's method was to link by patchcord a radio directly to the tape recorder. The radio was tuned to a suitable spot on medium wave between stations (interfrequency) that are transmitting to where only the rushing sound of white noise is heard. Jurgenson claimed the help of a mediator in the beyond named Lena and Dr. Raudive, for a brief period, also had a mediator named Spidola. If one seeks for the assistance of such a helper, one tunes slowly from one end of the wavelength to the other listening carefully for a voice that will whisper 'record now' or some similar hint. Then switch on the tape recorder. Later, on replay, all the extraneous noises of normal radio have to be eliminated so that any paranormal voices present can be studied. A more simple method in the radio technique is to tune the radio to a suitable frequency, say on medium or short wave between stations that are transmitting, but allowing a very modest mixture from the two stations. The tape recorder is not plugged directly into the radio jack, but a microphone from it is placed about five inches in front of the radio loudspeaker. I also plug headphones into the recorder and this allows me to monitor the whole proceedings.

'Of course one has to record in a quiet room free from distracting sounds but the open microphone method appears to give better results possibly by utilising room resonances. Although one can find more radio free spots on FM where white noise can easily be heard, researchers find this wavelength unlikely to produce results. A few have obtained paranormal voices on air-band but in one case it was discovered the radio had a technical fault and so in fact was receiving short wave, and in the other case normal aircraft to control tower conversation appeared to be paranormally voice modulated. As far as radio intrusion is concerned this is possible even when no radio is used.

'All kinds of electrical apparatus are capable at times of picking up radio signals which are everywhere. The mere presence of an unexplained voice on a tape recorder is no proof in itself that it may be paranormal. This can only be decided by what it says, if it is of someone recognised, or if you are addressed by name, and the context.

'When making microphone recordings the technique is exactly as for normal recordings except that the record level controls are turned to full volume. Most of my own microphone voices were made outdoors in the countryside, often by lakes since I found the quality of the paranormal voices improved when recorded by still water. Dripping water can also carry voices and I must stress it is not the acoustic illusion of words that can be often produced by the chance splashing of water, but actual whisper type voices that can be heard combined with these sounds. Splashing water produces numerous frequency combinations like white noise. Jurgenson claimed the best recordings were obtained during the summer months after sunset and in winter during dry cold weather, before sunset. He also said that the clearest and loudest voices seem to be on the night of a full moon. This could be a gravitational effect. Solar eruptions and northern light static disturbances also prevent voices from manifesting. He was sure the key to the whole electronic voice phenomenon is modulation of sound; sound which probably already exists or is created and then utilised. A carrier wave is also essential.

'According to Herr Koberle of the VTF EVP group, the largest in Germany, it is technically possible to use television as well as radio and also to use either speech or music as raw material to make up (pre-recorded) EVP test material. He says "I have left the tape recorder running during some television transmissions and had commentaries as interruptions, for example, when an actress went from the cash desk of a cinema into the cinema itself someone (on tape) whispered: 'She wants to see the film' and one time when I had to make a phone call during a fairly loud television transmission, someone said: 'Switch the television off'." All this indicates that the recording sessions are closely monitored by our unseen friends in other dimensions.

'It is, I believe, essential to record on a regular basis and the initial recordings should not last longer than ten minutes. First, after having decided on the technique you will use, introduce yourself by name on tape, stating the time, the date and the method and then ask to speak to friends in the beyond. After a few minutes, repeat this, giving your name again and asking if you can be heard and if so, whether the voice entities will say your name. If a reply is audible during this play-in you can frame your questions to respond, otherwise at the end of the ten minute transmission express your thanks and then rewind the tape and thoroughly check. A ten minute recording can take at least an hour to study and analyse. Once you have recorded your first paranormal voice you will realise the fascination this research holds and the important discoveries still waiting to be made.'

Inevitably the predication that the voices we receive on our tape recorders are the voices of the dead and/or extraterrestrials living in dimensions undreamed of leads us to a wider discussion of the whole question of mind and matter. If 'they' are speaking to us, where are they? This question of 'place' bugs me. Whilst recording for the EVP I ask time and time again: 'Where are you?' I never get an answer. George Bonner, on asking this question on one occasion, received the reply: 'In your own flat.' When I asked the same question, the answer – the one and only answer I've ever received to this question was – 'I'm praying.' What can I make of that? I debated whether 'praying' was a place, in the sense that place and time are one and the same thing in the world, or worlds, beyond. Or could it be that my communicant was so self-evidently in my house that a question such as 'Where are you?' was answered by what he was presently doing. Much as if you call from one of your rooms to someone in another room down the corridor: 'Where are you?' they might very well answer 'I'm just washing my hands' or 'I'm watching the TV.'

Sir Oliver Lodge, Principal of Birmingham University and President of the Society for Psychical Research from 1901 to 1903, an eminent scientist and one of the pioneers of radio and television (but perhaps best remembered as the inventor of the spark plug used in the motor car) – together with his

Sir Oliver Lodge, FRS.

contemporaries John Logie Baird and physicist Sir William Crookes, President of the Royal Society – always said the next world is another wavelength and maintained:

'The dead live in the etheric wavelengths which operate at much higher frequencies than ours. Our physical world is working on vibrations that are up to the speed of light. The etheric world operates at frequencies far in excess of the speed of light.'

Sir Oliver wrote in *The Outline of Science* published by George Newnes Ltd. in the 1920s:

'Hitherto we have known life and mind as utilising the properties of matter, but some of us are beginning to suspect that these psychical entities are able to utilise the properties of the ether too – that intangible and elusive medium which fills all space; and if that turns out to be so, we know that this vehicle or medium is much more perfect, less obstructive and more likely to be permanent than any form of ordinary matter can be. For in such a medium as ether there is no wearing out, no decay, no waste or dissipation of energy, such as are inevitable when work is done by ponderable and molecularly constituted matter – that matter about which chemists and natural philosophers have ascertained so many and such fascinating qualities. Physicists, chemists and biologists have arrived at a point in the analysis of matter which opens up a vista of apparently illimitable scope. Our existing scientific knowledge places no ban on supernormal phenomena: rather it suggests the probability of discoveries in quite novel directions. Any possible utilisation of the ether, however, by discarnate intelligences, must be left as a problem for the future.

'What appears to be certain is that life and mind require for their manifestation and terrestrial development some form of "material" in the broadest sense, and that there is certainly an interaction between mind and earthly matter. The two branches of knowledge, the study of Mind and the study of Matter have usually been dealt with separately; and the facts have been scrutinised by different investigators – the psychologists and the physicists. The time is coming when the study of these apparently separate entities must be combined, for it has always been a puzzle how there can be any relation or interaction between two such apparently diverse things as matter and mind.'

At the time Sir Oliver Lodge wrote this, only two sub-atomic particles had been discovered, the positive proton and the negative electron. The neutral neutron was not discovered until 1932. In 1981 Professor F. Reines published his work on neutrinos showing that the universe could consist of nine-tenths of invisible mass. The physicist Arthur Koestler said that the neutrino behaved like a ghost; it could pass effortlessly through any physical matter. Scientists have now discovered over 200 sub-atomic particles, some of them 'out of this world'.

Ronald Pearson B.Sc., a former British university lecturer whose speciality is thermodynamics and fluid mechanics, has recently written a book *Intelligence Behind the Universe*, with an accompanying appendix of mathematical proof, and a companion booklet *Colossus*. These argue the case for the cosmic force driving the phenomena of continuing life and in so doing, mathematically confirm the forecast by Sir Oliver Lodge and the experiments of Sir William Crookes and other researchers. Quoting from J. J. Snyder's booklet *Has Science Confirmed Survival?* published by The Campaign for Philosophical Freedom, Pearson sees post-mortem survival of the human psyche as one of the many functions of a three-dimensional, subatomic grid matrix on which all levels of life exist interpenetrating one another. The grid sustains the etheric as well as the physical consciousness of all living organisms.

Sam Nicholls B.Sc., an astrophysicist from Leeds University, England and a fellow researcher into sub-atomic phenomena, concurs with Pearson's findings. He has further postulated that so-called 'deceased' entities, although composed of slightly different atomic components, exist in and share the same space with the material world. He states: 'Like the physical universe, their world would likewise be composed of sub-atomic particles, but these may be in much closer vibrational harmony with the all-pervading 'grid' than their physical counterparts.' In one context of observation, the grid itself could be visualised as the Creator-Sustainer of a number of parallel, but separate universes. This premise does not, however, negate the possibility of an even higher ultimate intelligence behind the grid.

Another British researcher, astrophysicist Michael Scott B.Sc. of Edinburgh University, cites Niels Bohr's *Copenhagen Interpretation of Quantum Mechanics*, presented at a conference in Tomo Italy in September 1927, as seeming to actually require the existence of consciousness as a non-material extension to space-time. Scott makes the point that sub-atomic physics, as explored by himself and other researchers world-wide, no longer views the building blocks of the universe as discrete particles of solid substance, but rather as vague, wavelike structures whose existence borders on the ethereal. Scott further states:

'The advancement of quantum physics has produced a description of reality which allows the existence of parallel universes. Composed of real substance, they would not interact directly with matter from our own universe.'

Professor Fred Alan Wolf, although not a member of the British group, seems to concur with their findings in his book *Mind and the New Physics* in which he writes:

'Fantastic as it may sound, the "new physics" called quantum mechanics posits that there exists side by side with this world, another world, a parallel universe, a duplicate copy that is somehow slightly different yet the same. And not just two parallel worlds, but three, four and even more…! In each of these universes, you, I and all the others who live, have lived, will live and will have ever lived, are alive!'

These theses could explain where the voices we hear via the EVP are coming from – an unseen parallel universe vibrating at a higher frequency which is shadowing our own; a kind of negative of the positive, viewed from our earthly perspective, wherein 'dead' people with their personality, intellect and memory intact, can see us, hear us, read our thoughts and speak to us telepathically via mediums and by imprinting their voices onto magnetic tape. But *how*?

Thomas Edison, the scientist who invented the light bulb and the phonograph (the forerunner of the record player), declared in 1920 at the age of 73: 'If our personality survives (death) then it is strictly logical and scientific to assume that it retains memory, intellect and other faculties and knowledge that we acquire on this earth. Therefore if personality exists after what we call death, it is reasonable to conclude that those who leave this earth would like to communicate with those they have left here. I am inclined to believe that our personality hereafter will be able to affect matter. If this reasoning be correct then if we can evolve an instrument so delicate as to be affected or moved or manipulated by our personality as it survives in the next life, such an instrument when made available ought to record something.'

Is the tape recorder the instrument Edison was referring to?

Jurgenson believed the voices used something like radar to communicate. He said: 'I do not believe that recording results depend on the type of equipment used, for if the dead do not turn on their radar there will be no voices, or only very weak ones. The phenomenon is above any technical explanation that we know and makes a mockery out of our concepts of time and space. I also believe the ability to hear the voices depends not only on our ears but on our psychic sense too.' He stressed the influence of the moon and believed reception of the voices depended on electro-magnetism influenced by the magnetic fields of the earth.

George Bonner says: 'Perhaps they are a product of our own subconscious, as some parapsychologists believe, or are thought forms that have an independent existence from the mind that gave them birth. But if that is so, how is it that they appear to think and reason without a brain? Various PK theories have been advanced to try and explain this. I find it difficult to believe that my own mind conscious or unconscious, in some mysterious manner decided to fabricate all the different male and female voices I have recorded over the years in order to deceive or placate my ego.

'Many of the voices I record respond to me personally and even pre-empt what I am about to say and this leaves no room for doubt. For example, I usually introduce myself, when recording, by stating: "This is George Bonner calling in peace and friendship." On one occasion I had only go so far as to say "This is George Bonner" when a voice cut in: "Calls in peace and friendship." On another occasion I had just begun to say "Can you tell me...?" when a voice responds "The radio's talking to you." I asked "Can you say my name please?" and the response was "George Bonner." Another voice stated: "I can see you talking." During one recording I asked: "Shall I put the light off to see whether this helps?" On playback a voice was heard to say: "Not a spiritualist medium." I took this to mean that either I am not a spiritualist medium or that the electronic voice phenomenon was not the same as a circle in a spiritualistic meeting.

'For years psychologists have found the unconscious mind an ideal repository in which to unload unexplained phenomena and indeed, since it is hidden from our conscious self, its mysteries have never been fully revealed, even by the most thorough analysis. Even so there is no hard evidence to show that voices can be produced on tape by the human mind by extra sensory perception or psychokinesis even when ordered to do so under hypnosis, a state of altered consciousness where suggestion is at its most effective. Additionally, even if the "projection" theory that the voices emanate from the subconscious mind was pursued, having worked in psychotherapy during and after the war, I am familiar with these effects and there is no way in which we can mistake genuine voice phenomena for imaginary voices or hallucination. A hallucinatory voice, for one thing, cannot be copied onto another tape, a regular procedure in EVP. Whether we believe in survival or not it is very hard to remain aloof from such voices that after all could be striving to give us the vital information that all humanity has sought throughout the ages. Can we afford to ignore all the evidence and pretend that these voices are just projections of our own imagination and wishful thinking?'

Just as the road to hell is paved with good intentions, the road to heaven is a quagmire of extravagant elitist claims by people who assume proprietary rights over electronic communication with the dead which cannot be substantiated. Unlike the EVP, which is a repeatable phenomenon continuously expanding for all, ITC (Instrumental Transcommunication) is not. It has to be taken on trust. You must be a believer. One of its first proponents, George Meek, a wealthy retired engineer in the USA, became interested in the EVP in 1971 and was convinced sophisticated apparatus would enable him to make two-way high grade communication with the 'dead'. He met an electronic technician, Bill O'Neil, who was also a clairaudient and clairvoyant medium. The two formed the Metascience Foundation and solicited funds by public donation for their research, raising $\frac{1}{3}$ rd million. Mr. Meek invested $100,000–$150,000 of his own money. They invented a system named Spiricom. An entity named Doc. Mueller allegedly spoke through it. He told O'Neill he had died in 1967 and gave numerous facts to verify his identity. Long two-way conversations were held and recorded. Unfortunately, Spiricom only worked when O'Neill was present. After a while Doc. Mueller broke contact after telling O'Neill he would 'not be here for ever'. Mr. Meek never patented his device, which faded into obscurity.

CETL (Cercle d'Etudes sur la Transcommunication), a Luxembourg based group headed by two civil servants, claims to receive pictures of the dead on television screens, phone calls from the deceased (including Dr. Konstantin Raudive and others) and faxes and computer print-outs from spirits and angels. The group has an American arm and together they have formed an organisation called INIT (The International Network for Instrumental Transcommunication) which holds international conferences and elicits public funding. Messages that the organisation's leaders claim to receive from 'higher beings' via electronic means, couched in pseudo-philosophical language, are published in INIT's tri-annual magazine. In the thirteen years since its inception, the Luxembourg group's atypical phenomena have not been replicated by other researchers involved in technical spirit communication. The organisation has attracted cult followers, and because of this and the fact that their know-how has not expanded into the mainstream and is very different from the painful step-by-step accumulation of demonstrable evidence on the phenomenon experienced by most EVP researchers, many people consider it to be bogus.

People will always come along to muddy the waters in any area of serious investigation; paranormal research is no exception. The problem is the hoaxers usually grab the headlines whilst the body of genuine seekers and finders after truth plod on unremarked. Then there are the professional 'sceptics', people who usually know nothing about your subject and who have no intention of finding out anything about it.

George Bonner, writing about this, says:

'Critics of the paranormal continue to pour scorn on those of us who work and demonstrate the reality of psi phenomena. Most use the old time-worn clichés of psychology to back up their arguments, even when this goes against medical evidence as, for example the tried and trusted British TV sceptic Dr. Susan Blackmore's insistence that the out-of-body experiences are caused by an hallucinatory experience, the result of oxygen starvation. Consequently the public are at a loss to know what to believe. Living in a materialistic society they tend, in general, to become sceptical. To further confuse matters there have been those who claim psychic powers of one kind or another in order to cheat and defraud.

'However, in spite of this situation, one might have expected intelligent people who have studied parapsychology to have the ability to separate the wheat from the chaff, and to know what is genuine and what is spurious. This is especially important in the case of the electronic voice phenomenon which can be studied under absolutely controlled conditions, as it has frequently been over the past 35 years or so. There is no doubt whatsoever that these voices exist and can be recorded on tape, analysed by voice print and put on computer. I have recorded thousands of examples during 25 years of research. I fully admit that in our present understanding of the laws of electronics the phenomenon does not appear to make sense, but then neither does our concept of reality. Unless we move ahead to major new discoveries in physics, we will remain unable to take on board these new breakthroughs. Over the centuries man has been given signs, sent prophets, heard voices and seen angels. Whether they are real or hallucinatory is not the point. The question is "What is their purpose?" I believe reality and imagination can flow into each other. Everything is interrelated. Reality is, after all, a state of mind: of consciousness. Perhaps by the very act of observing, we create what we observe and give to it its own consciousness.

'A vast mindscape exists that is also part of our own psyche. It is not just tied to the physical gland, the brain, but is much more than that; indeed, consciousness may have created the brain. We must be open to all possibilities, for we live in a universe that is conscious and that therefore has meaning and purpose. Such ideas will be impossible to accept by those who continue to be tied to the old mechanistic and materialistic philosophy of science if one dare call it that.

'A totally new concept in fundamental physics has opened up in which matter and consciousness are seen as a single field. Man is now able to build a bridge to science, philosophy and healing. The role of transcendental voices is a major one and many are too afraid for their reputations, their jobs and their funding to go public and admit this fact. New doors to understanding the real nature of man are opening. We are the pioneers of it in the electronic age.'

Raymond Cass of Hull, Yorkshire, one of the few remaining dedicated EVP researchers in Britain, has retired from his practice as a hearing aid specialist and feels free to talk openly. Mr. Cass, who is bi-lingual German/English and worked in the German section of the Foreign Office after the second world war, says:

'The EVP controversy is more complicated than you can imagine. Phones are tapped, mail intercepted. Experimenters I know holding positions of responsibility keep quiet about the whole subject for fear of losing their jobs. I took part in a secret meeting at Schwalbach in Germany in 1980 where the possible repercussions on society at large were discussed. One prominent EVP researcher was convinced he could be a target for government hit squads. It has been said that the forces on the other side who transmit the voices have yet to decide how far to push the phenomenon in the light of possible reactions by governments. This implies powers held in reserve.'

He began researching the EVP after reading Dr. Raudive's book in the 1970s. He recalls:

Raymond Cass.

'There was great enthusiasm at that time and many experimenters but as it became clear that weeks or months of effort was necessary before a single voice came through, most people dropped out. Only a few survived – George Bonner and myself amongst five or six others. We eventually assembled a body of objective voices which clinched the case. However, the establishment ignored the evidence. The Society for Psychical Research were frosty; the Spiritualists relied on mediumship so the EVP people were pretty isolated.

'It is common knowledge that on the Continent progress was much more impressive. The Germans, with little access to mediums plus the ability to burn the midnight oil, soon had local groups going and some heavyweight technical research. Due to the language barrier there was little or no cross-fertilisation and the UK experimenters were, in general, low on funds and couldn't afford to take trips abroad. The subsequent progress in transcommunication went unnoticed in Britain. Very few understood any German and there was quite a bit of envy. My contacts with the Continentals dwindled away. Like the others, I couldn't afford trips abroad to investigate the situation. Meanwhile the Germans, stung by Cambridge chemistry student David Ellis's attack on the validity of the EVP in his book *The Mediumship of the Tape Recorder*, gave up the UK as a bad job and there was little contact.

'All efforts to design machines which would do the job mechanically failed whatever the cost – George Meek's 'Spiricom' cost in the region of £2,000: but here and there striking spontaneous voices appeared on tape. I myself accumulated over 1,000 clear voices and sold many compilation tapes which attracted much praise world-wide.'

Raymond Cass believe there are groups on the 'other side' who locate a target person and push material through for as long as the 'window' is open. Based on the evidence of his own 'voices' he says:

'They can do as they please providing conditions are right and no amount of concentration, prayer or wishing influences the result. Nor are they willing to disclose their modus operandi, or their location or ultimate intentions. It is not what the experimenter does or thinks; it is what is *done to him* by the mysterious forces. The entities are in possession of some advanced technology.'

Mr. Cass does, however, feel that his genetic background may be favourable to psychokinetic manifestations. One of his ancestors at the turn of the nineteenth century was a powerful physical medium, Robert Cass, and 150 years before that Molly Cass of Leeming, North Yorkshire had a hard time with her contemporaries and narrowly escaped being burnt as a witch and in fact ended up more than once being ducked in the village pond – a traditional punishment for women suspected of dabbling in witchcraft.

Cass' first 'other dimensional' voice came through at the age of seven. He recalls:

'I was alone in our large, rambling house overlooking Bridlington Bay, Yorkshire. I was reading war books in what we called the breakfast room. Downstairs we had a rather primitive radio with the old-fashioned horn speakers positioned in the upstairs rooms. The radio had wet and dry batteries but was switched off that day – my parents were out. Suddenly my name was called over the speaker at room volume. I raced downstairs but the house was silent and the radio off. There was no explanation for the male voice and the phenomenon was, according to the electronics of that day and age – impossible! Nowadays we know about VLF waves – very low frequency radio waves used by the military for penetrating distant and submerged submarines. Such a powerful impulse could energise the coils of the primitive speakers. But in 1928 who was transmitting VLF? No-one so far as we know. I realise now this was a precursor of my later abilities, but a mysterious intelligence was calling the shots.'

Eleven years later, at the age of eighteen, Raymond Cass was to come face to face with his destiny at a seance held by the Scottish materialisation medium Helen Duncan. In his own words:

'My first ever book from the Hull Public Library at the age of 13 was by psychic investigator Harry Price, which included some highly doubtful pictures of Duncan ectoplasm. The faces depicted looked artificial, and even grotesque. This naturally coloured my perception of Mrs. Duncan's powers in a negative way, and it was not until 1939 when by sheer chance I was offered a place at a Duncan séance that I was forced radically to alter my opinions. As a wartime evacuee from Hull to the coast, I occasionally attended the SNU church at Bridlington which was run by a local medical man, Dr. Hastings. Beyond a nodding acquaintance at the door with the principal, I was merely an anonymous young man; a casual visitor. Due to a last minute cancellation, a vacancy at the forthcoming Duncan seance became available, and I snapped it up.

'One night, November 28th 1939, Helen Duncan and her husband arrived over an hour late from York after a journey in thick fog and the 'blackout' (the compulsory switching off of car headlights, street lights and any other light source during the war). On arrival, they had a quick cup of tea and a nurse changed Mrs. Duncan into a one-piece black garment. (This was generally done to preclude the possibility of mediums concealing apparatus to defraud in their garments.) The séance was held in Dr. Hastings' home, in his oak panelled study under the strictest test conditions. The whole of the proceedings were in good red light and before commencing, each sitter expressed complete satisfaction that no loophole for fraud had been left. Mrs. Duncan, who was an 18-stone Glaswegian with a heavy, almost incomprehensible accent, sat in a 'cabinet' – a curtained off corner of Dr. Hastings' study. Her husband, a small, thin man, was in the audience together with the rest of us, mostly seaside landladies. I sat at the front.

'Unknown to anyone present, I had bought, the previous week, a second-hand copy of the *Rubaiyyat of Omar Khayyam*. It was a miniature, ornate, beautifully illustrated edition which was not discussed with a living soul, and disappeared into my small library at home. Mrs. Duncan's spirit control, Albert, announced: "This is curious. I have a gentleman here who has been on our side for a great many years, a gentleman of Persian nationality. He comes in a beautiful pink spirit robe and wishes to communicate with someone here. A young man sitting in the front row." After a few moments, the curtains of the cabinet parted, and a six-foot tall, majestic figure, clad in flowing ectoplasmic drapery and wearing a large headdress of unusual design, stepped out in full view of the sitters. He had a small beard. His face was extremely beautiful, the eyes deep set. In clipped cultured English the spirit-form spoke: 'Greetings from Omar Khayyam.' A learned dissertation

followed on the moon and the stars, and reference to my occult and philosophical studies, followed by some typical Eastern poetry, a blessing and an
invocation. The entity then retired into the cabinet. Albert (Mrs. Duncan's
control) announced from the cabinet I would develop voice mediumship
"through which the Persian gentleman will transmit to the world beautiful
prose and poetry." I very much doubted this as the war was soon to intervene.

'Throughout several years in German prison camps during the war, that
evening remained in my mind and still stands out as an inexplicable and
cathartic experience. Thirty years after it, in 1970, I became heavily involved
with the electronic voice phenomenon and recorded many hundreds of loud
and evidential paranormal voices. The prediction was fulfilled but not in the
way I expected.'

Before Mr. Cass retired in 1985 his main office in Hull seemed to attract
many clear and evidential voices to manifest on tape by the radio interfrequency method. He used a cheap Japanese multi-band Juliette radio and a
small pocket tape recorder. Over a couple of years the reception and quality
improved and his name was mentioned by the entities. He felt they regarded
his location (which was surrounded by a great deal of electromagnetic flux)
and his set-up favourable, and within the limits of their remit, were allowed
to put across significant evidence. In February 1974 a paranormal voice was
recorded at his office in Hull which, although striking enough at the time, had
an unexpected and confirmatory sequel late in 1980. Cass reports:

'It was my habit, every Tuesday, to leave the office in the care of my assistant Miss Ingrid Feuchte and to attend my sub-office in Scarborough, where
twice-weekly patients were seen, hearing aids fitted, routine repairs carried
out, etcetera. There was no telephone at this depot so I was ordinarily not in
communication with anyone in Hull. On this occasion Ingrid had told me of
her intention to hold a "play-in" if time allowed and this she proceeded to do
over the lunch hour. I gave her permission to use my office at the top of the
building where the Juliette radio and a portable cassette recorder were hooked
up by patchcord. With the monitor switched on the content of the recording
could be followed and if switched off, the session would proceed silently until
the end of the tape; usually a C60 (30 minutes one side). Shortly after this
particular session, though we were unaware of it at the time, a long and tire-
some negative period was to commence for reasons not fully understood to
this day.

'The radio was tuned to 127 MHz airband, where due to the absence of aircraft above the city, and of a local airport, there was usually radio silence apart from some mains and car ignition interference from the street below. Sufficient stabilisation of our contact with invisible forces had been established over a period to render it unimportant whether or not the experimenter held any particular mental "set", tried to concentrate, or merely switched on the apparatus and stared out of the window. Voices were routinely recorded at the rate of approximately six per hour regardless. These were rapid, abrupt interventions, arising without warning from the white noise background. They were in no way faint whisper voices requiring close study and concentrated attention. They were real vocal effects using polyglot speech, with sometimes strong emotional overtones and frequently lyrical and musical in format.

'Hearing the office bell ring below Ingrid left the set-up and dealt with the customer. During this time the recorder ran until automatic shut-off at the end of 30 minutes. By now Ingrid was obliged to deal with early afternoon clients and retrieved the tape about an hour later. She switched off the gear, stowing the cassette in her handbag without listening to it. Picking her up that evening at Bridlington railway station she handed it to me and we agreed to study the contents, if any, after the evening meal. Atmospherics, car ignition noise and the normal white noise hiss of the VHF band occupied the first few minutes of the tape then suddenly a high-pitched urgent male voice, heavily accented, shouted "Cass away – busy in Scarborough." There followed a bantering remark about Ingrid, then astonishingly "I must be scarpering." Following this, silence for two minutes, then the same voice: "Listen! Hoch Baba is slowly coming and teaches the world!"

'About a week previously Ingrid and I had read a book about the Indian holy man Satya Sai Baba by Howard Murphet. In 1974 the activities and the psychic abilities of Baba were only just penetrating to the West with a fraction of the publicity he has gained in the psychic and occult press since 1978. We were reasonably sure at the time that the voice referred to Sai Baba but did not associate this high-pitched machine-gun-like diction with the Saint himself. I had imagined a deeper, less excitable voice and more measured diction. The remark "Cass away – busy in Scarborough" I found remarkable. The polyglot insertion "Hoch Baba" (*hoch* is German for exalted) I found confirmatory of a paranormal origin: the voices use polyglot speech whenever possible, but I thought at the time that the claim "Baba is slowly coming" a little odd – a modest claim about the time factor. Three years later I was to read in Dr.

Sandweiss's beautifully illustrated volume on Baba that in an interview with the psychiatrist Baba stressed that the recognition of the Sai mission would only come about slowly: "Baba offers no instant solutions."

'However, here is the punch line. In late 1980 I read in a psychic journal that a Sai Ram centre had been established in the UK and that tapes, books, etcetera were available. I was anxious to hear Baba's actual voice, curious to hear the living expression of the holy man who by now, due to expanding publicity in the West, had advanced from the obscure figure of the early seventies to a well-known celebrity. I bought a few cassettes where Baba mostly uses an interpreter for his homilies on morality and religion, only occasionally bursting into a high pitched rapid-fire English. *But this was the voice on my tape of February 1974*: same pitch, same accent, same breakneck speed, same forceful declamatory emphasis.

'Extracting a typical short extract from the Baba tape where he plunges into English, I placed it in juxtaposition with the voice which came over 127 Mhz in February 1974. There was no doubt: the 1974 voice was the voice of Baba himself or a perfect simulacrum! It is claimed that Baba is aware of the thoughts and deeds of his devotees and potential disciples regardless of physical distance. Dozens of India's most eminent scientists, medical men, educators, generals and army officers testify to his pre-eminence as a potent spiritual force, living amongst us today, flaunting his psychic gifts, healing power and telepathic insight freely and unstintingly. Fortunately this particular voice sample was included in the tapes I issued during 1975 to 1977, of which there must be a few hundred still in existence, although at that time I included it as a good and interesting example, not realising that this rather testy voice could be that of the Swami himself. I still possess the original copies of the voice made that evening. This can be subjected to any comparative test or to voice print analysis.

'Despite the negative phase which supervened early in March 1974, I now regard this sample as evidence of the strongest calibre for the objectivity and genuineness of the EVP and more important, its staggering potential if stable avenues of reception can be identified and the requisite apparatus developed.'

But, despite evidence that most of the EVP communications appear to be from deceased persons (or, as in Baba's case, from a powerfully spiritual person still alive), Cass has a theory that some of the voices – loud, robotic, metallic – are from alien entities. He says:

'I resisted the idea that aliens might somehow be involved in the opening of channels to parallel worlds and other dimensions wherein reside the millions of our honoured dead. Today the explosion of UFOs, alien abduction and cattle mutilation stories in the media and, more recently, a glut of expensive and glossy magazines on the news stands with the images of 'Greys' staring from the covers, shows a public thirst for contact with advanced beings who might save us from our ecological sins and slide into self destruction.

'Both Raudive and Jurgenson were aware of the existence of a tougher breed of communicating entity on the other side operating so-called transmitting centres with names like Radio Peter and Radio Kelpe. These entities selected a few experimenters, seemingly at random, but were liable to switch them off without warning. The experimenter would assume he had entered a 'negative' period during which time no amount of concentration would evoke the voices. I still have a tape where an irritable voice told me: "We'll work the switches." In the same period a harsh male voice warned: "Carefully with the nerve gas." And a female followed with: "An evil struggle commences."

'In 1975 I incorporated these voices on a demonstration cassette sent to academic institutions in Japan and the USA. Twenty years later came the nerve gas attack on the Tokyo subway. Subversive forces world-wide preside over vast stocks of nerve gas. The warning should still be heeded.

'The concept that extraterrestrial forces can enhance communication between the dead and the living on earth will be anathema to many spiritualists and until recently I regarded UFOs and EVP as two separate phenomena. Now I am not so sure. Recently David M. Jacobs Ph.D., Associate Professor of History at Temple University, USA and a leading authority on alien interventions, when asked what governments could do about the situation, replied: "Absolutely nothing. The aliens have an incredibly advanced technology. They can do what they want to do, that's the bottom line!"

'To illustrate the above implications, a German EVP pioneer Frau Schmitz of Bottrop, recorded a voice predicting the time and location of a UFO appearance over Bottrop. In front of many witnesses two UFOs, brightly lit, appeared through low cloud cover over the city. Simultaneously, electrical and phone systems in the Schmitz household went completely haywire.

'To quote from Dr.James Deardorff, a senior government scientist, meteorologist and principal of the US National Centre for Atmospheric Research: "They (aliens/entities/the dead) would communicate with a few recipients scattered over the Globe. A recipient would be supplied with messages over an extended time period and would be allowed to gather extensive evidence of the reality of the voices so as to be able to gain some measure of public acceptance of the phenomenon." He reckoned that a very slow drip-feed over a period of years would be necessary as too rapid an incursion into the public domain would invite censorship and opposition.'

Clearly, Dr. Deardorff's fear of a too rapid incursion is unfounded. As Raymond Cass points out:

'It seems that dimensions overlap momentarily and the requisite conditions are rare. If you imagine two carousels rotating in opposite directions on a fairground and one person is attempting to shout to another across the space – only rarely will a message be conveyed. The EVP situation does not yield to logic. If it did, everyone would be at it.'

All is well

Everything in the barracks was mildewed. The journey back to Ireland had been stressful. Vic looked white and strained. I had the dull thumping warning on the left side of my head of a migraine headache. And every single item we had left in the house piled in one room so the plasterers could work was covered in greenish black in varying degrees of intensity. Even the pine doors stacked in a corner had a furry green membrane. The water from the drying plaster had been absorbed into the beds, sofa, rugs, books – all the pages mouldy, stained and stuck together. We hadn't anticipated this happening. We looked round with mounting dejection.

Bug emerged from somewhere deep inside the car. He'd been let out of his box en route, together with E.T. who, despite being tranquillised and unable to open his eyes, had yowled at regularly spaced intervals like he'd been wound up all the way to Swansea and most of the way from Cork Harbour to the house. He actually bit his way out of his box during the crossing. Woody was probably jammed under the seat. We left him to get out of the car when he felt like it, we were too worn out to look for him.

The floors of the rooms and corridors were mired in a thick mixture of plaster droppings and mud. My oak dining table had been used by the builders to stand on to plaster and it was now thickly coated in greyish-white. The chairs, despite my tying them all together as a not-so-gentle hint not to use them, had been untied and used, and now matched the plastered table. They looked like something out of The Flintstones. It was all too much. Our voices echoed round the empty grey rooms, our hearts sank. How could we start from scratch again? So much work! Unending!

That night, sleeping in the shed because it was the only dry place, I had a dream. It was of a man, an architect, standing in front of a plan chest, stooping to take long rolls of drawings from the drawers, spreading them out one on top of the other on the sloping top of the chest, and looking at them intently. I could only see his back so I didn't know who it was. I saw a black Rapidograph pen in his hand. I remembered the images clearly in the morning, but they didn't have any relevance to being in Ireland, sleeping in a shed. Later in the year I was to understand this dream.

The next day the world looked a brighter place. The sun came out and the buttery-yellow gorse covering the scarred land filled the air with a warm coconut-oil scent. There were more birds around – chaffinches and black-headed crows, a couple of bold robins, three magpies who chattered and scolded at the bottom of the bank like old women doing their washing by the stream. The pond had filled up with the winter rains and, amazingly, there were tadpoles – hundreds of them – darting round. Bits and pieces of greenery had sprung up here and there, at the edge of the pond and on the grey clay banks. Wild rhododendrons had flowered everywhere, their massy mauve heads jostling for space with the gorse and brambles. The eucalyptus trees seemed twice as big as they did last autumn. It was as though the land had breathed a sigh of relief when the builders and their machinery had left, and had slowly, gently begun to clothe itself again with its mantle of green, gold and mauve. We attacked the plaster dust and mud, dragged all the damp things out of the house into the sun and emptied the car. Woody was prised out from under the seat where he'd been all night and calmly walked into the house and started to eat as though nothing had changed. The next task was cleaning out the well.

Two weeks later Douglas, who'd agreed to be my P.O. Box for the EVP Society, sent me on some mail. There were twenty letters from people to whom I'd written, wanting to join the Society, enclosing their annual subscription. I'd told everybody the first newsletter would be in January 1997, when the Society would effectively begin. We were expecting to go back to England in November, in five months' time. I was very excited by this initial interest and started my list of members. As the weeks went by, more and more letters arrived and the membership grew steadily. Lots of people wanted the tape I'd made for the psychic weekend in Prestatyn. I had to keep buying 60-minute cassettes and copying my master tape. We'd bought a secondhand Sharp dubbing tape deck in London and brought it with us. It did a very good job, but on the occasions when I had twelve or more requests for the tape, it took hours doing them one at a time. I was happy, though, to know that people were interested in the EVP and looking forward to producing my first newsletter.

One day the words 'heart attack' came into my mind. All day long I heard myself mentally repeating them. I thought perhaps I was going to have a heart attack, or Vic (and the thought panicked me) – but he's too young. Then I thought it must be Helmut, our German friend. He was always working at full stretch and running around. He'd been dizzy sometimes, he said. I wondered whether to warn him, but knew he wouldn't take any notice even if I did, and it might worry him. The next day the words were still in my mind. And the day after, and for many more days. Then a Beethoven symphony started to play in my head. It was his Fifth. The melody was constantly there. I found myself humming it every day. It went on and on. I couldn't stop remembering it, in some detail, and I didn't even realise I knew it that well. He isn't my favourite composer. But I didn't add things up – heart attack and Beethoven's Fifth, and the dream of the architect. I don't know why, it was so obvious. Perhaps subconsciously I had put two and two together, because what happened in September wasn't entirely unexpected.

One very hot day in early June I drove to Bantry, the nearest town eighteen miles away. The evening before I'd been thinking about Paul a lot, missing him, wishing I had told him more than I did, how much I loved him. I wondered where he was and if, when I died, I would see him again. I felt very miserable. As I drove to the town he was at the front of my mind. I was even talking to him out loud in the car. When I got to Bantry I did my shopping, then walked down an alleyway I'd never been down before. It led to a narrow street lined with cottages all painted in different colours. As I came to the end of the alley I looked across the road at the cottage facing me. It was painted green. It looked rather neglected and the windows were very dusty. Scrawled in the dust in big letters on the ground floor window were the words 'Paul OK'. I stared at the writing transfixed. My mind flew back to Douglas in London. He had said, 'Does Paul ever use the word OK?' I had looked at him strangely. Now it made sense. Paul was OK. He was fine, or he was saying in that stroppy way he sometimes had, 'Look, mum, stop worrying about me, it's Paul – OK?' Whichever way I looked at it, the meaning was clear. I was elated.

Sitting for the EVP had been shelved for a while. But in July I set up the tape deck with its remote microphone and tried to get someone to speak, preferably Paul, but with the EVP you never know who, if anyone, will visit you. Vic was in the room at the back of the house hammering. It was raining and as I turned the tape recorder on I said into the mike 'It's raining,' and then continued talking, explaining where we were, the date, the time. Vic came into the room and we had a normal sitting, not as long as usual. When I played the tape back, where I said 'It's raining' a very faint man's voice echoed me:

'It's raining.' At the point where I'd finished the introduction, the same voice, but much clearer and louder, said: 'She says everything!' I presumed the 'she' referred to was me, and the remark had a certain edge of sarcasm to it, but we were very happy to have recorded these two comments and established contact in the Irish house.

After this recording, nothing happened psychically for some weeks. Admittedly we didn't record for EVP very often as work at getting the house into shape was all consuming. Vic began to make furniture, a hitherto unrevealed talent: a Sierra Madre style cupboard from an old door, a television table from the cut-offs of the work-top, a bedside table from an old bamboo bed headboard and an absolutely beautiful built-in bedroom unit. We had to buy the wood for this. After it was finished, we both looked at it in awe. It was so good.

I took on all the painting. It was horrible. The walls are rendered inside with a sort of grainy effect which needs twice the effort, and paint, to cover them. Magnolia everywhere! – I did the ceilings the same, it was easier. Acres of magnolia. I soon got sick of it and painted the bathroom in 'sea spray' aquamarine and the lobby in 'desert sand'.

Apart from the inside, there was the outside. It was a building site. All the ground for yards around was compacted cement dust on top of compacted grey clay. A raw, 15 foot high clawed-out bank ran for fifty feet in front of the house which had literally been built on a platform set into the side of a mountain. I couldn't see anything ever growing on this bank. It was like an archaeological excavation, revealing different strata of soil and rock formations all the way down to the Jurassic period. It only had a foot or two of top soil, the rest was blue clay going into red clay, all of it oozing water. The super highway from the road to the house looked like an extension of the motorway, viciously grey and barren. I clothed it in my mind's eye with chamomile and thyme, clumps of marguerites waving at the edges; an avenue of trees. It would take for ever!

By September the kitchen was operable. Vic made the worktops, fixed up the cupboards, wired up the electric cooker and plumbed in the sink. I'd done most of the interior painting and started on the outside. First I thought I'd paint it green, then pink, but in the hardware shop in Bantry I was irresistibly drawn to 'Renoir red' – rather like blood. Heidi and Helmut, who live at the foot of the mountain but can see the house from a field away, said after I'd painted the back of the house that they thought a fire had broken out, but it was only the setting sun making it look more vivid than usual. In the same month, we discovered the potatoes we'd planted in early June were ruined. They'd got blight. I thought that had gone out with the Irish famine. The leaves, which sprang with such vigour through the carefully earthed up ridges two months earlier, blackened round the edges, turned yellow and dropped off. The 'mother' potatoes liquidised in the earth into an evil smelling sludge and the babies had no chance to grow to adulthood. Too late, somebody told me I should have bought English seed potatoes as they've been certified disease free.

At the end of September Vic's father, my ex-husband John, died. We weren't told until one day before the funeral, which was in London. Vic tried to make arrangements to go, but there wasn't time. His premature death wasn't unexpected but it was still a shock. A few days later I realised I had been told in advance this would happen but hadn't added things up. In May I had a dream of an architect. John was an architect. I couldn't get Beethoven's Fifth symphony out of my mind, he loved Beethoven, his favourite. He had a bust of the composer in his flat and knew all his music note by note. I was mentally repeating the words 'heart attack' over and over. John had a heart attack. I knew, without knowing. I had attributed the signs to different people – myself, Helmut, Vic. Had I noted them in the order they were received, I would have made the connection. But, if I had, what difference would it have made? I wouldn't have been able to change destiny. John died on the 25th of September. On the evening of October 1st Vic and I were in the house watching something on television. Music by Richard Strauss began to play and Vic said: 'You like this, don't you? and John liked it too.' At that exact moment all the power in the house went off like a switch had been thrown and instantaneously came back on again. I had already experienced spirit intervention with electricity and both of us were positive John had been with us at that time and had caused the power to be cut momentarily as an indication which we could understand, that he was there. Later, looking through the notes I had made of my sitting with the medium Rita Rogers in June 1993, I read that she forecast John would die in eighteen months. She was eighteen months out in her prediction.

If we had not accumulated the knowledge we had over the course of the four years since Paul died, I know Vic would have been devastated by his father's death, despite the fact that he had seen very little of him since he was seven years old. The growing conviction that in some miraculous way not yet understood, some part of us – a sentient part – lived on, helped us both to see his death as simply moving on to another dimension. The incident with the electricity being turned off reinforced our conviction. When we recorded for the EVP after this, we included him and asked him to speak. Unfortunately, we weren't getting any answers from anyone since the occasion when the man in July had said 'She says everything.' There seemed to be an EVP embargo. Whilst in London, even when we were recording a lot of voices, we noticed how random the phenomenon is. If you are successful at one session, having noted all the constituents which might have a bearing on that success – weather, moon's cycle, equipment used, who present, location, etcetera, and you duplicate the experiment exactly on another occasion, you invariably get nothing. So it's impossible to aggregate the possible factors and arrive at a workable hypothesis.

One of the reasons I was so keen to form a society was in order to be able to draw the threads of research into the EVP together and hopefully find common ground on which to build. Douglas was sending me regular large brown exciting envelopes full of letters, many from would-be members and my waiting list was growing. Meanwhile, the letting agent wrote and asked if we would like to renew the tenancy on the London house for a further six months. After some hesitation we agreed. The social isolation was already affecting us and we realised that when the house was finished, it would be more evident. But, looking round, that still seemed quite a way off, and the money would help.

In December there was a psychic breakthrough. Vic had a theory about the microphone we were using for the tape deck. Something to do with impedence and oscillation. I am not technically minded and am quite happy to try whatever combination someone who is so minded suggests, without trying to understand the reasons why. He suggested using the micro-cassette recorder for EVP instead of the standard cassette deck, as it had a higher impedence mike. I had abandoned the small machine in the belief that the standard deck (in imitation of the one which had recorded the discarnate American lady's voice) would produce better results. So for our next sitting we used the small recorder with the Sharp as a back-up. We positioned ourselves in a room we hadn't yet tackled. It was empty, undecorated; no curtains, no carpet, very little furniture. I mention this as the possibility of room resonance being a contributing factor to receiving voices had been discussed by other experimenters. When I asked the question, on tape, 'Is it right that a high impedence microphone is better to receive voices?' the answer we received on tape on playback was a loud emphatic man's voice saying 'Exactly!' When this voice was transferred from the small recorder to the large cassette to log and preserve it, another voice interjected during the transfer with the words 'That's it!' We seemed to be on the right track of encouraging the entities to speak to us in Ireland. And the voice on transfer was a new development. It had obviously used the ambient sound wave produced by the micro-cassette to record onto the cassette in the larger tape deck.

Christmas arrived again. The cake I'd made was eaten a month before, so I made another. That got eaten in advance as well. I bought the usual turkey at the last minute. Whether it was because I didn't put my glasses on or because the giblets were inserted into an unusual orifice in the bird, I left them inside in their plastic bag and roasted it. The kitchen filled with a faint sickly smell and our appetites diminished throughout the cooking process. We couldn't work out where this smell was coming from and eventually decided it was to do with the oven not having been used before. I didn't even find the bag until I'd carved the meat and put it on plates. It looked grisly. A roasted piece of PVC with some shrivelled objects inside nestled into the turkey's body. The whole experience put us off eating it and off meat in general for months. Not only were potatoes blighted; looking back over the past four years, Christmases were blighted too. Only the birds and a stray ginger cat who appeared outside the door on Christmas Eve enjoyed the 1996 one. New Year's day was very cold indeed. The ground was frozen hard, so was the pond. Hard enough to throw large stones which made an impact disc, then skittered across to the other side. A few hours later the discs had frozen into large milky pearls. On peering through the ice, we could see reeds which had begun to carpet the bottom, trapped upright in an icy green still-life.

On January 13th 1 experienced something I couldn't explain. I awoke suddenly and looked at the clock; it was 6.25 in the morning. My room was pitch black. I had had one of those restless nights, unable to sleep, tossing and turning. I had only got to sleep an hour earlier. As I looked up towards the ceiling I saw with surprise that the whole area was canopied in black lace covered in a raised intricate design made from what looked like chenille velvet. I looked very hard at the design, trying to make out exactly what it was. I could see inverted musical notes – treble clefs, bunches of reeds and intricate geometric shapes. I pinched myself to make sure I was awake – I was! I closed my eyes and opened them again. The black lace canopy was still there. I could see through the lace, yet the room was in complete darkness. It didn't fade or change in any way as I stared at it for about ten minutes, trying to make sense of it and impress it on my mind. I switched on the light. When I switched if off the canopy had gone but it had been replaced by a sort of lightweight light grey fisherman's net which gradually faded. I thought very hard about what this could mean; what symbolism, if any, it had; how this vision had been created and why. But I couldn't find an answer at the time. Some months later when the house in London was sold, it did strike me as interesting that the buyer was a Mr. Reed who was a musician.

It was time to compile my first newsletter for the EVP and Transcommunication Society. I'd been gathering items together for months and now they had to be welded into a form which would introduce the subject to the uninitiated and not bore the people who were further along the road. The EVP is a phenomenon which draws you inexorably into technical realms whether you like it or not. I asked two friends, Dr. Tom Keen D.Sc. and Gerry Connelly B.Sc., both members of the Society whom I had got to know through correspondence, to act as its scientific and technical advisers. I was very pleased when Colin Smythe, who had initiated the first controlled scientific tests on Dr. Raudive's material, joined too and agreed to become the Honorary President. I printed one of the letters I'd received some months earlier in my first newsletter, as it accurately reflected the pain and joy of recording for the EVP. It also noted one of the characteristics, which we had experienced ourselves, of a voice appearing either right at the very beginning or end of a tape. The letter was from one of the members, a Mr. William Cunliffe who lives in Austria. He wrote:

'It eases my sense of chagrin a little to know that you too, have erased voices: although it still hurts to think about it, as I have a very strong feeling – but no evidence of course – that this was the one voice above all others I was anxious to hear. Since writing to you I have had but one single voice which came through about three weeks ago although I have been trying two and three times each day. This particular recording was made in the evening about 11 pm and I was using a new tape. My usual method is to switch on the radio – for the white noise – then switch on the recorder, and after a slight pause, start recording. However, on this occasion, I must have switched on the recorder first, before the radio, paused for a few seconds as usual, then started to speak. At the end of the recording, which usually lasts for some 10 to 15 minutes, I rewound the tape in order to check and right at the beginning of the tape, before I had started speaking, were two very loud knocks and then an audible voice, not a whisper as before, which said either "Er macht was falsches" or "Er macht es falsch." It is quite distinct, yet not distinct enough to determine whether it is the former or the latter sentence, although the meaning (he is doing it wrongly) is the same in both. The only difference is that the former is the Viennese idiom, whereas the latter would be more grammatical. Either way it is saying that I am doing something wrong. This time I did not experience the cold sensation which I felt with my first – erased – whisper. I was probably too amazed to feel anything. And then came the doubts – had I knocked on the table myself, had I picked up a radio station; was I imagining this voice? So I asked a friend who is also interested, to listen to the tape and tell me if he could hear anything. He had to listen several times, but he finally told me he could hear "Er macht was falsches." I pressed him to listen again and tell me whether it was really that, or something slightly different and eventually he, too, came to the conclusion that it was either one or the other. I very nearly erased this too – but caught it just in time. (I have since adopted a method so that this cannot happen again.) I did erase the two loud knocks; however, as they were not part of a message, I don't feel too badly about this. And apropos knocks: I have since tried to reproduce them by knocking on the same table on which I make the recordings but they don't sound at all alike, so I must assume they too came from the same source as the voice.

'But, as I said, that was about three weeks ago and since then there has been nothing, and I've been trying now for about five months. If I am doing something wrongly I wish the voice had elaborated a little. I follow the instructions on your tape; I have read and re-read the methods employed by Raudive and seem to be getting nowhere. The fact that I've had two messages in five months is rather like getting three numbers correct in the lottery: just enough to keep hope burning but not enough to feel elated.'

Mr. Cunliffe carried on trying and wrote to tell me that several months later he recorded fourteen different messages during a session with his brother and sister-in-law. One of those voices appeared on tape during the time they broke off for dinner. He believes one was the voice of the dead person he most wished to hear from – the one whose message he had inadvertently erased. In his letter, he mentioned recording the message "Er macht was falsches" right at the beginning of a new tape, during a brief pause before he switched on the radio. This meant that although he was intending to record using the radio interfrequency (white noise) method, he had actually picked up the voice by the open microphone method – the one I use most of the time. The fact that the voice was imprinted onto the magnetic tape immediately after the tape recorder was switched on correlated with some voices I had received either at the beginning or end of tapes and with Vic's theory on the build-up and break-down of a magnetic field as an inducement to capturing voices. Apparently when you switch a recorder on or off you create high voltage and low current in an expansion and breakdown of the magnetic field. George Bonner also noted this and advocated what he termed 'a wobble effect' – switching between stations on the radio. This creates a breakdown and setting up again of two opposite fields and makes sense of his recommendation to use back-ground noise as a carrier wave for the voices, as water, bells, bird song etc. are in themselves the breaking down of sound carrier wave fields. This also goes some way to explaining why so many of the voices that researchers into the EVP receive follow immediately on their own. Our voices, too, produce thermal energy and create the same field. None of this, of course, explains exactly how discarnate voices imprint onto magnetic tape and where the owners of these voices are. That was what I wanted the Society to discover.

Voices were now imprinting on our tapes, using the micro-cassette recorder. On the evening of February 4th, I was alone in the house and decided to do a quick recording for the EVP but first made myself a cup of tea. I drank the tea and poured out a second cup which I took into my bedroom, with the small recorder. Sitting on the edge of my bed drinking tea, I chatted away for a few minutes into the machine, then switched off and played back. I was surprised and delighted to hear a woman's voice come in over the recorded sound of my gulping tea. She said pleasantly: 'Two cups of tea Judith!' I knew who it was. I recognised the voice. It was my half-sister Miriam, one of the first batch of children of our extended family, who was a great deal older than me, and who had died shortly after Paul. She had an obsession for making several cups of tea from one tea bag with the result that everyone got a cup of tea so weak it was virtually undrinkable. My brothers called it gnat's piss. We all used to laugh about this trait of hers. It was a very valuable and interesting message. First, I recognised her voice; secondly the comment indicated she was aware I had drunk a first cup of tea in the kitchen and was on the second and thirdly, she had chosen to make a remark about tea, as a reminder of the joke we had at her expense, thus providing perfect evidence that it was her. The words also conveyed the fact that her memory was intact, she could see me, and she'd kept her sense of humour – and her accent (she was educated in Lancashire in the north of England).

Immediately after receiving this message, I went into the sitting room and switched the television to 'mush' in order to provide a carrier wave and magnetic field. I had read something that Herr Koberle of the largest German EVP Society, the VTF, wrote about comments he received via the EVP whilst he was watching television and recording. I also tried something else: asking my question while recording, then switching the recorder off slowly and on again to see if the entities could interject into that breaking field. Using this method I asked: 'Was it Miriam saying "Two cups of tea Judith"?' The instant reply heard in that tiny gap on playback was: 'Of course!' The voice was male and very pompous as though I was inane to ask such an obvious question.

I immediately set up the equipment to transfer this message and Miriam's to my standard-size cassette. When I had done so, I played the cassette over and discovered two more voices had imprinted, as they had done on an earlier occasion, during transfer. One, a woman's, said: 'Typical!' and a man's voice said, in a peremptory tone: 'I'm talking to you!' I was elated that the voice entities seemed to have forgiven us for deserting London and retreating to the backwoods for so long.

On the evening of February 22nd there was a full moon. Friedrich Jurgenson had written that the full moon, because of its gravitational effect, seemed to encourage voices to manifest. It was a wild night, raining and very windy. There had been hailstones earlier. We set up the equipment in the same empty room as before, using the small recorder and the Sharp deck as a back-up. We switched on a Sony Airband radio tuned to 108 MHz as a carrier wave. Vic left the room to fetch an adaptor and I said, with the two micro-phones recording, 'Vic's gone to get a…' then couldn't think of what he'd gone for, so left the sentence hanging in mid-air. Vic returned, and later on during the session I tried the switching off and on technique that had captured the voice of the man replying 'Of course!' when I asked about Miriam. On playback we heard a man's voice which I had begun to recognise, at the point where I'd said: 'Vic's gone to get a…,' finish off my sentence by saying 'micro-phone … wheatstone.' Vic explained that 'wheatstone' was a kind of sensitive electrical circuit. At the section where I had turned the tape recorder off and on again, we were startled to hear a very loud woman's voice with a mid-European accent state: 'Ian – back home!' The phrase 'back home' is often used by spiritualists to denote a person's passing over, but even bearing this in mind, we knew only one Ian – the man in Douglas' circle who kept a cattery and who we suspected of helping the phenomena along. We certainly didn't bear him enough ill-will to want to attribute the statement to his early demise, wonderful evidence though it would be. But interestingly enough, the next letter I received from Douglas said Ian was in hospital, seriously ill.

Immediately we heard the two paranormal voices we transferred them to the special cassette as usual, as a precaution against their deteriorating. When we played that cassette back to check they'd recorded properly, in a gap between my saying 'Vic's gone to get a…' and the male entity adding 'microphone … wheatstone' a woman's clear voice had interjected in a chatty tone, during the transfer process, 'Not cold enough, is it?' We instantly recognised the voice with its intonation and distinctive Lancashire accent as that of Nana, Vic's paternal grandmother who had passed away some years earlier. The remarkable thing was this direct answer was in response to a *thought* Vic had at that time about the weather, and if it would hail again.

February was a good month. On the 13th Vic and I were talking about buying a computerised typewriter. I'd been lying in bed the night before thinking about how I was going to produce the next newsletter for the EVP Society. My old portable which was immensely hard work, giving me repetitive strain injury, was on the table by the window with a fresh sheet of paper rolled into it. Vic was by the fireplace and I was on the other side of the room in the kitchen area, cooking. The cats were not in the room. As I was stirring food in a pan I said to Vic: 'Do they make typewriters any more, even computerised ones?' He replied: 'Yes, of course they do!' and at that exact moment there was a loud crack from the typewriter. It sounded as if a thumb and forefinger had flicked a taut piece of paper very hard, yet the paper in my machine was drooping forward over the keys. We looked at each other and laughed. The decision was made. Two weeks later a Sharp FW-750 personal word processor was sitting on the table, baffling us with its Japanese complexities until Vic cracked it.

On the 28th Vic used an experimental crystal microphone for the first time, sent to us by Dr. Tom Keen. Tom's theory was that a normal mike works on converting sound waves into electrical charges whereas a crystal mike doesn't solely depend on soundwaves but more on electrostatic charges present in the air around and is possibly more sensitive to the EVP. Vic said the usual 'Recording-one-two-three-four-five-six-seven' into the mike, using the small recorder. On playback the 'five-six' had disappeared to be replaced by John's (his father's) voice saying urgently: 'Vicks!' John always added an 's' onto 'Vic' to make a nickname, and the voice and manner of speech was absolutely his. It was unmistakable. Encouraged by this first-time result, we used the crystal mike the next time we recorded, and the time after that, but got absolutely nothing.

The next full moon was on March 24th. Remembering the success of the last session on the night of a full moon in February, we set ourselves up to record. But this time there was only one voice. It appeared in an unlikely place on the tape during a period of silence (other than the hissing of the radio 'white noise'). It was a woman who said in a conversational tone, 'That's Paul's mother.' Who she was, who she was conversing with, is a mystery, like the EVP phenomenon itself. The voices, coming from nowhere, open a door to the unknown to allow a tantalising glimpse, then shut it again before you have a chance to ask any questions or learn too much. The fact she had mentioned Paul made it even more frustrating. I was beginning to wonder if we were meant to know more than that they are real and that they exist – somewhere. The next day, recording on my own, I asked the man (I estimated twenty-five to thirty years old) who had spoken in February on the night of the full moon saying 'microphone ... wheatstone' to speak to me. I named him Mr. Wheatstone. I tried several short recordings of a few minutes each. On playback, as the machine was switched on for the last attempt, he spoke. It was the same light south of England voice. He said, in a whisper: 'Keep on talking.' I reiterated loudly: 'It's you I want to keep on talking!' I think he heard me!

The EVP was temporarily abandoned for two weeks after this as the builders descended again to fit doors and architraves and deliver stones, sand and cement for the wall to be built at the entrance to the drive which, incredibly, was no longer grey and austere. In such a short time it had coloured with clumps of wild clary, saxifrage and vivid green cushions of moss. Reeds and buttercups were growing by the small stream running alongside it. Grasses of all descriptions waved on the banks which had not long ago been churned up mud. Even some of the willow cuttings I'd given up for dead had rooted and sent out strong stems of bright green buds. The ravaged land was repairing itself and wearing new clothes. April 14th was the next time I managed to record again. I switched on the Olympus and after a while of reflecting out loud how many voices we'd had on the night of the full moon in February and looking through my diary for the next full moon which I found was on the April 22nd I said to Mr. Wheatstone: 'Where are you? I wish you'd tell me.' I played the tape back immediately and heard Mr. Wheatstone's instant, enigmatic reply: 'I'm praying.'

The next day I received a letter from one of the Society's members who told me George Bonner, one of the doyens of the EVP, had died on April 8th. I knew George was very ill and had mentioned it in the Society's April newsletter which had just gone out. I had received a letter from him only two weeks earlier telling me how ill he felt after two heart attacks and a stroke and asking me not to forget him. As if I could! I'd replied straight away. I wondered if Mr. Wheatstone's answer the evening before I learned about George's passing had anything to do with it. Was he praying for George? George had told me, despite his twenty-five years of recording thousands of EVP voices and the cumulative evidence they had provided of an after-life, he still had doubts as to whether there was life after death. I hoped he now knew the answer.

Mid-April; the gorse out in full bloom again, the air filled with its warm sweet scent. The weather was like the south of France; streams dried up, grass began to yellow. A vast blue dome of sky streaked only by vapourised jet-streams from planes flying to and from the United States, too high up to see. The passengers' view as they looked down on the west coast of Ireland through cloudless sky would have been idyllic: tranquil emerald glens, gentle uplands embroidered in dark green rising to purple jagged crests of ancient volcanoes softening and fingering out into the Atlantic. A few cars with holidaymakers passed by. As they slowed at the top of the mountain where the road flattens out ready for the final climb to tunnels cut through the rock separating Counties Cork from Kerry, the people in them peered down at us and at the magnificent panorama behind us. Life could be sweet again.

A week later, recording alone, I asked Mr. Wheatstone: 'Try and speak to us. Some people seem to have amazing contact, unless they're lying.' A woman's voice replied: 'Next weekend.' This was a new voice and I assumed her to mean contact would be made next weekend and accordingly recorded again on both the following Saturday and Sunday. Nothing happened on Saturday. On Sunday I left the recorder running while I went out of the room. When I returned I said to Mr. Wheatstone: 'Where are you? Are you here with me in this room?' Then I went over to the other side of the room and stroked one of the cats. On playback all I could hear on this tape was the sound of my footsteps going out of the room and a variety of other muted movements: then footsteps returning, and some other small sounds. Suddenly, perfectly clearly, an Irish woman's voice says: 'Mary.' There is silence on the tape for a few minutes, then Mr. Wheatstone whispers: 'Don't slam your brains.' I assumed he meant 'stop fussing over where I am all the time. I'm here.' It was quite comical to hear the quaint way he put it – almost Bertie Woosterish. On the heels of this command, the same Irish voice imprinted earlier saying 'Mary' urgently says: 'Help me out – now!' I was galvanised by the desperation in her voice. Who is Mary? Where is she? How can I help her out? I recorded and played back for hours and hours, trying to get Mary to speak again and give me some more information, but no more voices came on tape that day.

• • •

Who do these voices belong to? Where are they? What does their intervention into the electronic circuitry of our era suggest, and how do they do it? To answer the first question, I believe they are the voices of the dead. The evidence points to it. Voices categorically state they are the dead: George Bonner heard 'Convinced the soul exists' 'Raudive here – finish' and 'We are the dead' to quote three out of hundreds he received on the same theme. Paul finishing Vic's sentence, my father calling my name, my sister Miriam commenting on cups of tea, Vic's grandma; these voices are real, and they are the voices of people I couldn't fail to recognise, who have died. The voices also demonstrate they belong to sentient beings with personality and memory intact. They are sometimes humorous, sometimes ironic, brusque, plaintive, commanding, laconic, friendly; the whole range of human emotion is shown by the things they say and the way they say them.

In the twenty-five years he researched into the EVP, hundreds of voices addressed the late George Bonner by name: 'Hey Bonner – help you but a time', 'People love George' and his most famous voice: 'Bonner looks quite ridiculous' (when he had slipped to the floor asleep). The first voice I unintentionally recorded said my name, 'Judith'. That one word alone, by its spontaneity and context, alerted me to the existence of the phenomenon. The woman saying in an interested, conversational manner, 'That's Paul's mother,' implies so much. I am known, the speaker knows Paul in their present dimension, he has conveyed to her who I am, our relationship is accurately reflected: I was being observed.

The voices are not auditory hallucinations. Hallucinatory voices cannot be copied onto another tape nor heard by other people. As for the suggestion they could be a product of the unconscious mind projected and recorded onto magnetic tape by psychokinesis, I reject this out of hand. As George Bonner, a qualified psychologist and hypnotherapist stated: 'If a person under hypnosis, the most impressionable state of mind, cannot be induced to project his thoughts into a tape recorder, then it is hardly likely you or I in our normal state of consciousness could do so. And there is no supportive evidence to show that thoughts, conscious or unconscious, can be heard as audible voices even if we suppose some additional PK-type energy.'

The PK projection theory also presupposes that our subconscious can project, regardless of our gender, voices of either sex of all ages and nationalities in a variety of languages, and perfectly imitate voices of known personalities expressing thoughts, comments, information and ideas often alien to us. As Bonner says, 'It would be a case of the super-ego deluding the ego and projecting these delusions in clearly audible form onto magnetic tape in a tape recorder. I would say that in itself would be a miracle.' Also, how would the fact that one's consciousness (and subconsciousness) which invariably, when recording, keenly wishes to receive a voice on tape, is so often disappointed? If the voices were instigated by us, we would get something every time. Samuel C. R. Alsop, author of *Whispers of Immortality*, said: 'EVP is objective acoustic reality. I can dismiss PK easily. For example, if EVP amounted to PK which is thought transference from the researcher to the tape recorder in some unique way, then the tape recorder would only manifest the voice utterances which form the mental content of the researcher, and this doesn't happen. I can give you an example. I once called on tape for Margaretha Petrowski and a female voice returned with 'Alsop – Petrouska' – using the correct pronunciation. That, in my book, gets rid of TPK.'

I too believe the voice entities are existing in their own right. They speak when they want to or when conditions make it possible.They answer questions, make comments pertinent to situation or activity, they can read our minds and they observe us even when we are not recording. They have imprinted onto tape under strictly controlled laboratory conditions before a sceptical audience of professional people and scientists, and their voices have been analysed by voice print spectogram. Famous scientists of the past were convinced of the reality of spirit communication by instrumental means. Marconi, Edison, John Logie-Baird, Tesla, Sir William Crookes and Sir Oliver Lodge were all working to try and demonstrate it publicly. Thousands of people world-wide are also convinced that EVP voices are real and not the product of our imagination, and are trying to develop instrumentation which will prove to the rest of the world the existence of discarnate intelligences speaking to us from another dimension.

Where are they? This is the question no-one has yet been able to answer satisfactorily. I think they are here, with us, existing in a parallel universe which we can't see; they, however, can see us and seem oblivious to the fact we can't see them. I can't speculate on the form the voice entities take. I haven't had personal experience of materialisation to be able to say they are in human form, as they were on earth. It seems reasonable to suppose (assuming people who report having witnessed spirit materialisations of their loved ones or ghosts are not liars), that the voices we receive by the EVP are simply those of people who once lived on earth and who, if we could see them, would be instantly recognisable as human beings. On the other hand, without real evidence, it could be that in another spiritual dimension in a parallel universe, there is no need for a body (unless for purposes of recognition) and that the voices exist in their own right in some condition of time and space I couldn't begin to imagine.

A scientific explanation for the existence of an invisible dimension which could be inhabited by spirits has been given in David Ash and Peter Hewitt's book, *The Vortex*. It is based on Einstein's formula $E=mc^2$ (energy equals matter to the speed of light). This shows that matter (m) is equivalent to energy (E). As matter and light share a common movement, the speed of matter must be the speed of light. Science is agreed that everything in the world is composed of atoms and molecules. The vortex is the swirling of those atoms and molecules. The authors argue that the speed of the swirling of the vortex must be the speed of light and it is for this reason – the vortex swirling at the speed of light – that we can see things on earth. But they ask: 'Why should the speed of the vortex's movement be limited to the speed of light? Once its movement *exceeds* the speed of light then a person or thing will enter into super-energy, into a new dimension – a new world. But in this new world, the person or thing will be as solid as we are on earth. The only difference will be the vortices are swirling at a faster speed than when on the earth plane.'

This could explain where the voice entities are: in a different dimension vibrating, or swirling, at a higher frequency and thus invisible to us. It still doesn't explain why we are visible to them. How do the voices manifest on magnetic tapes? I think this currently is the hardest question of all and the best answer would be to simply say I don't know. I don't think anyone else researching the EVP knows either, or we would all have heard about it. It appears to be a miracle. Certainly the EVP doesn't obey known laws of physics. It breaks all the rules. The constituents for obtaining voices via the EVP appear to be: one's own psychic ability, recognised or latent, good hearing, perseverance, suspension of disbelief, and an open mind. The type of equipment used seems immaterial, except in so far as its auditory qualities are concerned. It's extremely difficult and wearing to listen for voices against a background of high internal microphone noise caused by poor quality components.

What does the intervention of the voices into our electronic gadgetry indicate? It indicates to me confirmation that spirits have always been amongst us but it is only now, by using an icon of our age, electronics that they can prove once and for all that they exist. Mediums can and do give irrefutable evidence of an after-life to the individual, the person who hears, as we did, information which could have come from no other source but the spirit world. Seeing a ghost is proof that something more exists between heaven and earth than mechanistic science would have us believe. A materialisation of a loved one, looking, speaking as he or she did on earth, assuring us we would join them when it was our turn, that they were waiting to welcome us to the dimension they exist in after death: this would be sublime.

But these psychic experiences are selective and subjective. However much one would like to be a party to them, there is the constraint of not having had the experience yourself. With the best will in the world you cannot help but speculate on the total validity of what they claim to have witnessed. The electronic voice phenomenon is not like that. It is exalting, mystical, mystifying but evidential and repeatable. The only one of known psychic phenomena which is. And this is why it is the Cinderella of the paranormal and has largely been ignored by mainstream psi and scientific researchers and the media. Professional scepticism is so entrenched, 'normal' paranormal occurrences so easy to debunk, that the EVP, presenting as it does irrefutable evidence of the existence of sentient beings in other dimensions, invisible to our eyes, but audible to our ears by means of electronic equipment in nearly everyone's home, is a threat to the continued credibility of those who will not see or even listen or those who may have comfortable elitist views about heaven.

There may be some electronic component, not yet formulated, which will translate the EVP from today's miracle to tomorrow's everyday occurrence: picking up the phone and dialling 'M' for mother in the beyond. Paradoxically, it may seem, I hope this doesn't happen. Much as I long to hear and see my son again, I am prepared to wait until the day of my final departure. The mystery should remain. We should not conquer everything as everything we conquer seems to be diminished. I can't think of anything worse than paying some international telecommunications conglomerate's charges in order to have the right to speak to my son in Paradise. I prefer to remain with my conviction he is there and one day I will see him again. In the meantime I will speak to him and he will speak to me using the electronic voice phenomenon, freely, in our own time, as and when whoever or whatever created the Universe sees fit.

How you can experiment with the EVP

The open-mike method

You need: A *tape recorder* (variable speed is useful as some of the 'voices' are very fast and need slowing down); *a new tape*; *a remote microphone*, if your tape recorder will take one, which should be hung up somewhere for maximum efficiency (a remote mike helps cut down background hiss); *a quiet room* and, very important, *a positive, expectant, cheerful, loving attitude of mind*. My personal experience has led me to believe a micro-cassette tape recorder tends to pick up more voices than a standard size one. I'm still not sure why this is. Without getting too technical, the reason could be that the smaller the electronic component, the higher the frequency it operates at and when you have higher frequency, there is greater energy being produced – in other words magnetism, and magnetism seems to play a considerable part in helping to capture and/or transmit the voices.

You may wonder why attitude of mind is so important. With this experiment, we are marrying technology and the paranormal. EVP is still in its infancy. No-one is yet able to determine what the constituent factors for its success are, and in what proportion. One's own psychic ability; a temporary suspension of disbelief in things other than material; a focusing on those loved ones who have passed on; equipment, location, persistence; discarnate choice; weather; all may play a part. On the subject of weather, Friedrich Jurgenson obtained his best voices in the summer after sunset (I endorse that). In the winter dry, cold weather before sunset produced best results. The loudest and clearest voices were obtained during a full moon which has a gravitational effect. I endorse this too, as several of my best voices including those of my sister who had died two years previously and my mother-in-law who had died seven years before were captured on tape during a full moon – two of them during a full moon and a thunder storm (masses of electricity and magnetism!).

To go back to the beginning: Having assembled your components and placed yourself (yourselves) in a quiet room, preferably with few or no soft furnishings and an uncarpeted floor (resonance seems to encourage reception), put the tape in the machine. If using a remote mike, place it in a free hanging position nearby. Set the counter on the tape recorder – this helps locate specific points on tape on playback where voices could have appeared. Turn tape recorder to 'Record', turn volume control high. Don't hold the tape recorder, put it on a table or on the floor. Introduce yourself. State date, time, location, weather conditions (for future comparisons). Speak loudly and clearly. Don't talk on top of each other, don't interrupt. Try not to cough or mutter or make any other noise at all as each little sound is picked up on the tape and on playback is easily mistaken for something else. If extraneous sound is heard, make a point of mentioning this on tape. Say you are present to try to make contact with friends on the other side. If you know someone who has passed over, address them personally. Ask them to speak to you. With the open-mike method, you will not hear any discarnate voices at the time of recording, only on playback. Leave gaps in your own speech in order for there to be space for a response from the other side; however, having said that, voices can jump into the tiniest space imaginable and often come in on the heels of your own voice or sometimes behind it. If you feel like singing, do so. Singing raises vibrations and creates resonance. Experimenters often report hearing someone extra singing along with them. I have heard this myself. Record for 10 or 15 minutes; although there is no time limit, a shorter tape is less of a strain to listen to later. Listening intently and interpreting sounds on tape is very tiring.

Play your tape back. Listen very carefully. At first it's hard to distinguish anything other than the background hiss of the tape recorder (which you can never completely eliminate) and the sound of your own voice. As the discarnate voices usually imprint at a level below that at which we expect to hear them you have to try to listen to all levels on the tape – listen through it. This is extremely hard at first, but becomes automatic later on.

The voices can be whispered. At first they usually are. They are sometimes very fast, often curt, often seemingly banal in their utterances. There is great economy of words yet what is said usually has more than one meaning. Sometimes prepositions and auxiliary verbs are left out. Usually one to three words are imprinted at first. If you hear something that may be an 'extra' voice, run the tape back and listen again – and again. *Don't make things fit*. If you are not certain, dismiss it. When you are sure you have recorded an 'extra' voice, transfer it to a 'holding' cassette or CD if possible. Listening to the voices you record at a later date is fascinating as what might have been a little obscure at the time of recording may suddenly make sense, or having become EVP-accustomed, you may hear something you didn't hear before. Also, transferring the voices saves them from being taped over or rubbed out.

The radio method

Follow the same procedure as before but include a *radio* in your equipment. The type doesn't seem important although some people feel *battery* operated ones are more effective than mains, and *airband* radios useful in that it is easier to find empty positions on the dial. Tune the radio to your chosen frequency. The aim is to find an interfrequency position – between two stations, where all that is produced is what is termed 'white noise', a gentle undulating hiss. George Bonner used Jurgenson's frequency of between 1400 and 1600 kHz. Raymond Cass uses 127 MHz VHF, although he says that with the over-crowded airwaves of today it's very hard to find an empty space. When the discarnate voices break through there is no mistaking them for ordinary radio transmissions as the free static sound is altered to a different pitch and recognisably modulated into words. At first these may be so soft as to be unintelligible. But persevere. This method, of course, enables you to hear the entities speak as they come through. Sometimes a short two-way conversation is possible.

You may get results at your first attempt, you may get nothing. Many people who now receive regular communications via the EVP tried for months, sometimes years, before getting anything. Vary your recording sessions by including other people, especially someone you believe to be mediumistic. I have found that when I record with a friend who claims he is not a medium but I believe is, I invariably get louder clearer voices. However, please don't be over-ambitious. There is no *guarantee* you will be able to record discarnate voices.

Try to do your recordings at the same time on the same day in the same room each week. Continuity and commitment seem to be important. It's only too easy to get discouraged if week after week nothing happens, but with perseverance I believe it will. The electronic voice phenomenon is real. It's a miracle, but it's real!

Well, that's it! The rest is up to you. Good luck and good listening!